CONNECTICUT FAMILIES OF THE REVOLUTION

CONNECTICUT FAMILIES OF THE REVOLUTION

American Forebears from Burr to Wolcott

MARK ALLEN BAKER

THE
History
PRESS

Published by The History Press
Charleston, SC 29403
www.historypress.net

Unless otherwise noted, all images courtesy of the author.

First published 2014

Manufactured in the United States

ISBN 978.1.62619.664.3

Library of Congress CIP data applied for.

To Elliott Mark Baker, the first son of Aaron Anthony Baker, who is the first son of Mark Allen Baker, who is the first son of Ford William Baker, who is the second son of Robert Roy Baker, who was a son of Ervin Baker.

In Memoriam

Ford William Baker, James Buford Bird and Flavil Q. Van Dyke III

CONTENTS

CONTENTS

Preface

We have it in our power to begin the world over again.
—Thomas Paine

A dozen generations now separate us from the American Revolution—a war triggered by resentment at the economic policies of Great Britain, particularly the right of Parliament to tax the colonies, and by the exclusion of the colonists from participation in political decisions affecting their interests—yet in the northeastern part of this country, on the beautiful coast of the Atlantic Ocean's Long Island Sound, rests one of the original thirteen states, where even today if you put three historians in a room and gave them the task of listing one hundred popular colonial surnames for the region, it would take only minutes. Names like Adams, Backus, Bacon, Baldwin, Bassett, Beebe, Beecher, Benedict, Bissell, Boardman, Brace, Bradley, Brown, Buel, Bulkley, Bull, Burr, Butler, Canfield, Catlin, Cheney, Chester, Clark, Cooke, Collins, Deming, Denison, Edwards, Ellsworth, Fitch, Goodrich, Goodwin, Gould, Grant, Griswold, Hale, Holmes, Hooker, Hopkins, Humphreys, Hunt, Huntington, Hyde, Jackson, Johnson, Jones, Landon, Lathrop, Lewis, Loomis, Lord, Lyman, Marsh, Norton, Ogden, Orton, Parsons, Paterson, Peck, Perkins, Peters, Phelps, Pierce, Porter, Putnam, Rankin, Reeve, Rockwell, Rogers, Russell, Sanford, Seymour, Sheldon, Sherman, Skinner, Smith, Stevens, Stone, Storrs, Strong, Tallmadge, Taylor, Thompson, Tomlinson, Tracy, Treadwell, Trumbull, Wadsworth, Ward, Webb, Webster, Whittlesey, Williams, Winship, Winthrop, Wolcott, Wood,

Woodruff, Wooster and Wyllys still send patriotic chills up our spines. This ancestry has become part of a Connecticut culture that takes pride in knowing that we have not lost sight of their dreams, forgotten their achievements or ignored their tremendous sacrifice. Out of respect, they endure. They are the Connecticut families of the Revolution: American forebears from Burr to Wolcott.

Acknowledgements

This introductory work owes a debt of gratitude to a wealth of individuals and institutions.

To the staff at The History Press: Tabitha Dulla, Dani McGrath, Vincent Vitali, Mattie Sowash, Magan Thomas and Will Collicott, I am so very grateful.

To the Connecticut Daughters of the American Revolution (April Staley, Alice Ridgway) and the Connecticut Society of the Sons of the American Revolution (Herman Charles Brown and Stephen Shaw), thanks for keeping the memories alive.

My sincerest appreciation to the following Connecticut towns and historical sites: Brooklyn, Coventry, Derby, Hartford, New Hartford, Hebron, Lebanon, Litchfield, Lyme, Middletown, New Haven, New London, Norwich, Stratford, Windsor and their town managers; the Oliver Ellsworth Homestead (the Connecticut Daughters of the American Revolution Inc., as a subsidiary of the National Society Daughters of the American Revolution); the Nathan Hale Homestead (Beverly York, site administrator); the Huntington Homestead (Scotland, CT); the Peters House (Hebron, CT); the Reeve House and Litchfield Law School (Litchfield, CT); the Governor Jonathan Trumbull Home (Cece Messier, Nancy A. Merwin); and the Noah Webster House (West Hartford, CT).

My gratitude to the following Connecticut historical societies (listed alphabetically): Ashford Historical Society; Connecticut Historical Society; Hebron Historical Society; Lebanon Historical Society Museum and Visitors

Center; Litchfield Historical Society (Catherine Fields, executive director; Jessica Jenkins, curator of collections; and Megan Olver, educational assistant), which includes the Reeve House & Law School; Ingraham Library; Wethersfield Historical Society; West Hartford Historical Society; and Windsor Historical Society.

Also to the following libraries/museums: the Library of Congress, the National Archives and Records Administration (NARA), the New York Public Library, the Smithsonian Institution and the Beinecke Rare Book & Manuscript Library, Yale University, New Haven, Connecticut.

I am indebted to the many wonderful independent bookstores of Connecticut, including Books & Boos in Colchester, CT (Jason Harris); Monte Cristo Bookshop in New London, CT (Christopher and Gina Jones); Bank Square Books in Mystic, CT (Annie Philbrick, Patience Banister and Julie); Byrd's Books in Bethel, CT (Alice Hutchinson); and the Nathan Hale Schoolhouse in New London, CT (Stephen Shaw and Debra Dickey). Also, my gratitude to Larry Rifkin (WATR), Ray Bendici (*CONNECTICUT Magazine*), Jason Grube (The Travelers), Dana Beck and Brian Brinkman, Venus Lusk, Kelly and Dennis DiGiovanni, Ann and Mark Lepkowski and Paul Mancuso (The 'Cuse).

My thanks to my family: Marilyn Allen Baker, Aaron, Sharon and Elliott Mark Baker, Elizabeth Baker, Brad and Rebecca Baker Lane, Richard Long and Cyndie Long.

It was a member of the Beecher family, Henry Ward Beecher, who said, "The unthankful heart…discovers no mercies; but let the thankful heart sweep through the day and, as the magnet finds the iron, so it will find, in every hour, some heavenly blessings!" Alison Long Baker has my thankful heart and is my heavenly blessing.

God Bless Our Connecticut Families

SECTION I
In the Wake of Revolution

Chapter 1

AFTERMATH

On September 3, 1783, the final Treaty of Paris concluded the American Revolution.[1] Details—from the recognition of a new nation and its boundaries to even fishing rights—had been arduously negotiated, and it was now time to evacuate all British troops and establish new navigation rights.

While the talks had been amicable, a point of contention was the "Loyalist question." The Crown, as expected, wanted its rights protected and confiscated property restored. However, the Americans disagreed; the Tories, as they saw it, were traitors. Finally, it was resolved that the states would "correct, if necessary," any acts of confiscation involving the estates of British subjects.

Connecticut, having already begun the process of repealing the wartime economic and military laws, celebrated the news formally with the termination of Council of Safety meetings in October and informally inside the town taverns across the colony. The American Revolution had transformed a monarchical society, where colonists answered to the Crown, into a republic—no longer subjects, citizens, primarily male, white property owners, could now actively participate in the political process. It was indeed a time of hope, even if it came at a substantial price.

FINANCIAL CRISIS

Plagued by massive inflation—not only was there continental currency to contend with but also that of individual state bills, with little backed by "specie" (gold or silver)—and war debt, the new federal government was powerless; it had no authority to levy direct taxes under the Articles of Confederation. In 1786, Congress convened in Annapolis, Maryland, to discuss the issue of interstate commerce. The result was a call for an authorized assembly.

The following year, fifty-five delegates, with George Washington as their elected head, put forward their governing ideas at the Constitutional Convention, held in Philadelphia. Two alternative structures emerged, the Virginia Plan and the New Jersey Plan.

Calling for a central federal government consisting of a bicameral (two-chambered) legislature—an executive branch and a judicial branch—

Some of Connecticut's finest politicians once walked the interior hall and stairs of the Old State House in Hartford. *Library of Congress*.

Virginia's solution also included a chief executive elected not for a term but for life. The resolution further called for the head of state to be elected by members of a legislature not equal but proportionate to state population.

Objection to the Virginia Plan (revolving around the power and tenure of such a chief executive, and a legislature tied to residents) was swift. Retaining most of the Articles of Confederation, including equal representation of each state, the New Jersey Plan added a separate and independent Supreme Court.

As the debate intensified, Connecticut delegate Roger Sherman stepped forward and proposed what historians would later call the Great Compromise. His plan called for a bicameral legislature in which the "upper house," or Senate, would represent states equally and the "lower house," or House of Representatives, would represent states proportionally by population. A strong chief executive would also be included, but he would be elected by an electoral college rather than by legislative members. Finding the proposition acceptable, William Samuel Johnson, along with Alexander Hamilton, Rufus King, James Madison and Gouverneur Morris, went off to style the final document.

POLITICALLY SPEAKING

Connecticut became the fifth state to ratify the new Constitution on January 9, 1788. And despite the new changes, the state remained on its conservative path. Oliver Ellsworth and William Samuel Johnson were selected as the first two senators for the state in October. Since the Federalists dominated the political stage, opposition was scarce. The state's initial delegation of representatives consisted of Benjamin Huntington; Roger Sherman; Jonathan Sturges, a lawyer from Fairfield; Jonathan Trumbull Jr; and Jeremiah Wadsworth, a wealthy Hartford businessman.

In February 1789, Connecticut's presidential electors—Governor Samuel Huntington, Lieutenant Governor Oliver Wolcott, Thaddeus Burr, Matthew Griswold, Jedidiah Huntington, Richard Law and Erastus Wolcott—unanimously cast their votes for George Washington. The vice-presidential ballot differed, with five votes for John Adams and two for local favorite Governor Samuel Huntington.

The Federalist Party—which dominated the state except for the most remote counties—held the governor's office until May 8, 1817, when Oliver

Wolcott Jr., a former Federalist and member of the Toleration Republican Party, was elected. Gideon Tomlinson, a Democratic-Republican, succeeded Wolcott in 1827. Organized by Thomas Jefferson and James Madison in 1791–93, the Democratic-Republicans, or Jefferson Republicans (also Republicans), opposed the Federalist Party and began their political domination at the turn of the century. National Republican John Samuel Peters became the governor of Connecticut in March 1831 when Governor Tomlinson resigned from office.

MIGRATION FROM CONNECTICUT

After 1783, there was substantial migration from Connecticut, western Massachusetts and Vermont into central and western New York.[2] This trend continued after 1800 and was typical of later relocation into the Northwest Territory. Western expansion, as a result of the Louisiana Purchase (territory sold by France, comprising the western part of the Mississippi Valley and including the modern state of Louisiana) of 1803, doubled the area of the United States. The restless and malcontents typically led the way, followed later by farmers and mechanics. Churches, mills and meetinghouses were quickly erected as entire communities took on an air of permanence.[3]

After the War of 1812, settlement interest shifted farther west, into Ohio, Indiana and Illinois. New York's population had increased from 340,120 in 1790 to 959,049 by 1810, much of it (estimates as high as two-thirds) originating from New England. The migration led historian Washington Irving to form the St. Nicholas Society, or "Old New Yorkers," if you will, to combat the growing New England social influence.

WAR OF 1812 (1812–14)

In June 1812, the United States declared war against Great Britain. This conflict was prompted by restrictions on U.S. trade resulting from the British blockade of French and allied ports during the Napoleonic Wars and by British and Canadian support for American Indians trying to resist westward expansion. As New England sentiment might have it, the entire Connecticut congressional delegation voted against the declaration.

When President James Madison issued a call for militia troops against Canada, Governor Griswold refused, declaring the request unconstitutional. Despite the independent minds of both the General Assembly and that of the governor's office, Connecticut citizens did serve in the armed forces, including about 1,800 officers and men in the regular army alone. As for the state, it remained untouched until April 1813, when a blockade led by British captain Thomas Hardy threatened its shores. Although under constant fear, only two notable Connecticut attacks took place: the first at Pettipaug Point, Essex, and later, in 1814, against Stonington.[4] As with any war, heroes emerged, such as Captain Isaac Hull and Connecticut's adopted son, Thomas Macdonough, while some faded, such as William Hull of Derby.[5] A treaty, which restored all conquered territories to their owners before the outbreak of war, ended the conflict.

CONNECTICUT'S MIGRATORY INFLUENCE

Connecticut's influence was far-reaching and more significant than many realize. For example, in Alabama, the Huntsville Female Seminary was organized by Miss Frances Strong. Like a few from her staff, she had been recruited from Miss Catherine Beecher's school, the Hartford Female Seminary. In Michigan, William Woodbridge, born in Norwich, Connecticut, became governor in 1840. Also, Isaac Crary, born in Preston, Connecticut, became Michigan's first congressional representative and defined the state's educational system. In Ohio, Western Reserve College was modeled after Yale and chartered in 1826 (it's first president was Dr. George E. Pierce, Yale class of 1816). In Texas, Moses Austin, born in Durham, Connecticut, traveled to Spanish Texas and received a grant allowing him to bring three hundred families to Texas. Unfortunately, Moses died before he could execute the grant, which he left behind for his second son, Stephen, known as the "Father of Texas." In Wisconsin, well, of the first eighteen governors of the state, four were born in Connecticut.[6]

As for the migratory influence of an entire Connecticut clan, one need look only as far as that of Reverend Lyman Beecher, whom we will detail in the chapter on the Reeve family of Litchfield. His family influence

Above: The Bacon Academy (as it looks today), in Colchester, where Stephen Fuller Austin, known as the "Father of Texas," spent part of his education.

Left: Mathew B. Brady's portrait of Presbyterian minister Lyman Beecher. *Library of Congress*.

spread to the Lane Theological Seminary in Cincinnati, Ohio; Illinois College in Jacksonville, Illinois; the Independent Congregational Church of Elmira, New York; the Second Presbyterian Church in Indianapolis, Indiana; and female colleges in Burlington, Iowa; Quincy, Illinois; and Milwaukee, Wisconsin.

Religion and Family

Religious beliefs played a pivotal role in the intimate relationships that shaped eighteenth-century American families. Early New England kinsfolk epitomized the broader Puritan priority on hierarchy, order and values; rights and duties were given to each family member by the head of household, who also saw to their sanctity. This spiritual tribalism—a conviction expressed brilliantly by Yale University professor Edmond S. Morgan in his landmark work *The Puritan Family*—assured the longevity of the church. As parental control over the economic future of the family weakened, so, too, did this patriarchal trend; authority ran parallel, for example, with the subdivision of the family farm.

Many studies have been made linking different religious persuasions to child rearing and gender roles. In author Philip Greven's *The Protestant Temperament*, he proposes that three styles of life emerged among Americans between the seventeenth century and the mid-nineteenth century: "evangelical," as exhibited by the Baptists, Methodists and Puritans; "moderates," less preoccupied with human sinfulness than the evangelicals; and finally "the genteel," a more affectionate and reassuring approach. Author Laurel Thatcher Ulrich in *Good Wives*, a study of women in early New England, documents the common role of that region's matrons as "deputy husbands" who were empowered to act for their spouses on a variety of financial and legal matters. Other studies go so far as to posit that some men still harbored dark suspicions of all women, and this misguided misogyny had made Connecticut women susceptible to charges of witchcraft during the seventeenth century.[7]

Throughout the colonial period, the missionary soul of the Congregational Church remained unmatched. From founding towns and schools to building churches, this Connecticut spirit even sent delegations to Vermont and into New York (1774). In 1800, *The Connecticut* evangelical

A second-floor interior view of the First Congregational Church in Litchfield. *Library of Congress.*

magazine was established as an official channel to stimulate interest in these home missions.[8]

For early New England settlers, it was not atypical to view marriage as a civil contract rather than a religious union. This trend, which included the social ideal of arranged marriages, slowly diminished, and by the end of the 1700s, love had become the dominant factor of a union. This being said, it will surprise few to learn that so many affluent Connecticut families linked through matrimony. High mortality rates, however, shortened the length of many marriages (the average length of a wedlock fell in a range between a decade and two decades in length and was dependent on a variety of conditions) and often led to remarriage, particularly when large families were involved.[9] Thus, it was also not uncommon for a child to lose a parent before he or she reached adulthood.

As for children, they, too, paid a price. Infant mortality was high, with many (quoted as high as 30 percent) never living beyond their first year and less than two-thirds reaching their teenage years. Puritan minister and prolific author Cotton Mather is an unfortunate example, as he witnessed eight of his fifteen children die before age two. As expected in an agrarian society, large families were the norm—the more available farmhands the better. Some colonial children were also "put out," or sent to other families to serve or apprentice for the new family providing for their needs.

As They Pass

On July 4, 1826, former presidents Thomas Jefferson and John Adams, fellow Patriots turned adversaries, died within five hours of each other.[10] They were the last surviving members of the original revolutionaries who could stand no longer with the British Empire.

In Connecticut, when the news reached Governor Oliver Wolcott Jr., then serving his last months in the state's highest office, he took it hard. He had been one of Adams's "midnight judges," appointed on the eve of Jefferson's 1801 inauguration. As a distinguished member of one of Connecticut's foremost families, Wolcott had witnessed firsthand the incredible transition in the state. In 1790, after serving as state comptroller, the population of Connecticut was just 237,946; it was now approaching 300,000, which it would reach during the following decade. He had seen the gradual reduction of a "rural" population (by 1890, it would be less than half). And he had also witnessed some of his recommendations, issues in which he firmly believed, fall on the deaf ears of the General Assembly. The ideology of his world, like that of so many other American Revolution family members, had changed. As the last surviving member of George Washington's cabinet, and the only Connecticut statesman, Oliver Wolcott Jr. passed on June 1, 1833.

Chapter 2

WOMEN, FAR MORE THAN
A FOOTNOTE

*If particular care and attention is not paid to the ladies, we are determined to
foment a rebellion, and will not hold ourselves bound by any laws in which we
have no voice, or representation.*
—*First Lady (1797–1801) Abigail Adams, wife of John Adams*

For over two hundred years, the American Revolution has endured
the scrutiny of experts (economists, historians, political scientists,
psychiatrists, sociologists…the list seems limitless), and while the slants differ,
most offer similar conclusions regarding the powerless.[11]

To disregard the sexism and racism exhibited by those in power before,
during and after the revolt would be a historical injustice. The role of
American women, like that of Native Americans and blacks, benefitted little
as a result of the insurrection. And they were not alone, as there was also
little merit seen in propertyless white males and indentured servants. Even
though together they represented a majority, jointly they lacked the control
of white propertied males. Left ineffectual, they had little choice, even after
the war, but to fill low-status functions. The only aspect of colonial life that
remained consistent for women was the Western European ideology of
subordination. Centuries removed, this subservience remains a disgraceful
truth, and one that many feel still hasn't been corrected.

An Unprecedented Opportunity or Simply Consequence

Women in Revolutionary days filled a large space in life, but a very small space in print. The heroic deeds of many a woman have slipped down into silence.
—*Sarah Preston Bughee*[12]

Family dynamics seldom remain constant during a conflict, and such was certainly not the case for the American Revolution. Women—not only educators, camp followers, protestors and caregivers but also daughters, sisters, mothers and grandmothers—managed themselves, children and even the family's farm or business. As indefatigable as this sounds, it was. But ultimately these responsibilities—or sacrifices, if you will—did not offer lasting political change, excluding women from the right to vote and serve in office. As deplorable as this resonates, it occurred.

Filling the "small space in print" has often been the formal names of Abigail Smith Adams and Dolley Todd Madison, both first ladies; playwright, essayist and poet Judith Sargent Murray; author Susanna Haswell Rowson; and a caretaker, Margaret Hill Morris. Lesser-known names—Patriots like Margaret Corbin, Deborah Sampson, Mary Hays, Nancy Hart, Lydia Darragh and even "Connecticut's own Paul Revere," Sybil Ludington, who rode through the countryside on a chilly April night and proclaimed that the British were burning Danbury—are occasionally recalled, but not at a frequency that satisfies most.[13]

Thankfully, organizations such as the Daughters of the American Revolution have seen to the resurgence of the roles of their predecessors, as well as to the resurrection of some of those who have slipped down into silence.

As the perfect prelude to the prestigious Connecticut families that follow, enjoy a selection of four unforgettable ladies, women of extraordinary courage and patriotism who will forever alter your view of the "Spirit of '76."

Eunice Dennie Burr

At the age of thirty, Eunice Dennie married Mr. Thaddeus Burr of Fairfield, a Yale graduate, a grandson of Chief Justice Peter Burr and a man who

The Thaddeus Burr Homestead in Fairfield was rebuilt after the devastation. *Library of Congress.*

would distinguish himself in public service. From selectman and justice to member of the Constitutional Convention and presidential elector, Thaddeus Burr became one of New England's leading citizens. As such, it's not surprising to learn that the Burrs entertained often in their Fairfield home, and on numerous occasions with their very good friend John Hancock of Massachusetts. In fact, the governor married Miss Dorothy Quincy of Boston at the Burr home.[14]

When the British attacked Fairfield (forces commanded by the menacing General William Tyron) in 1779, Mrs. Burr, who was home alone, would not yield to the enemy. Even as a dozen arms-bearing men sprang through her front door and inquired as to the whereabouts of her husband, she remained taciturn; it wasn't until the presence of the commander himself that she would orally renounce her assailants. The British wanted not only whatever papers and documents she had but also the comfort of her estate. With penitence and little recourse, she met their demands.

Subjected to the grossest indignities, Eunice Burr was simply beside herself. Having endured continual verbal and physical abuse since her capitulation, she gallantly addressed both General Tryon and Captain Chapman, a Tory citizen of Stratford who now sided with the British. "See that I am treated with the respect and consideration due my sex and station. See that my

From this entrance hall of the Thaddeus Burr Homestead, Eunice greeted her guests with the utmost in New England hospitality. *Library of Congress.*

home is preserved from further spoilation, and that the few people who have fled to my protection are saved from the abuses which have already been heaped upon me!"[15]

"You must carry a bold heart Mr. Chapman," Mrs. Burr firmly asserted, "to have the audacity to enter my house as an invader, when you recall the many courtesies we have extended to you in years past." Mrs. Burr, all too familiar with her assaulters, would not relent. To watch over the premises, an indisposed General Tryon then commanded sentries placed at her door.[16]

As the horrors of the evening unfolded, Mrs. Burr could smell the gunpowder, hear the screaming and feel the vibration of nearby shelling. From her window, she watched as house after house was set ablaze. Toward morning, Eunice Burr was again greeted by the megalomaniacal Tryon, who confided to her—perhaps out of a bit of contrition—that he would not burn churches, meetinghouses or the Burr home. Standing bravely, Mrs. Burr proclaimed with dignity her gratitude for such discretion. But even Tryon's directive was not enough. A horde of British cutthroats entered the home, and although she screamed that an order of protection had been given her personally by the general, they looted the residence and tore the gold buttons from the very dress she was wearing. As Eunice Burr fled to the safety of a nearby meadow, she watched in horror as the mansion was set ablaze and left to burn.

Having entertained the great and gifted of the land, from Benjamin Franklin and Roger Sherman to Lafayette and General Washington, all with a dignity and grace befitting one of the finest women of her day, a valiant Eunice Dennie Burr had been unwavering in her loyalty to both her husband and her country.

LUCRETIA SHAW

Through the artistic genius of American painter John Singleton Copley, the beauty of Lucretia Shaw was forever captured in a timely portrait. Donning a rich attire, and in perfect posture, her stately presence boasted an unmatched refinement, making it not so difficult to imagine her capturing the heart of Nathaniel Shaw—or any man, for that matter.

The elder Nathaniel Shaw had a son by the same name in 1735. And like his predecessor, the son became an eminent trader. So gifted would be the younger's maritime knowledge that, following the Battle of Bunker Hill, John Hancock himself penned the authorization of Nathaniel Shaw, Esq., as "Naval Agent" for the continent. The distinguished commission surprised few in New London, as many knew the mariner through his conspicuous association with the Sons of Freedom and their patriotic actions.[17] It was Shaw who had dispatched his own sloop, the *Queen of France*, to the West Indies to purchase some of the scarce gunpowder used at Bunker Hill.

In reality, many vessels saw and benefitted from Shaw's outfitting, both state and privately owned. He was active in Commodore Ezek Hopkin's first naval expedition sent out by the continental government. Relentless was his passion to equip his craft with the finest Salisbury cannon (during the conflict, the furnaces in Salisbury would cast over eight hundred cannon and become essential elements in the defense of Connecticut's coastal towns).[18] Besides his naval efforts, Shaw acted as an agent for the disposition and award of naval prizes and for prisoners of war.[19]

As for Lucretia, she was at the epicenter of the hostilities. Received at the Shaw home in New London were everyone from Governors Trumbull and Griswold to Generals Greene and Washington.[20] On the

An exterior view of the Captain Nathaniel Shaw Mansion at 11 Blinman Street in New London. *Library of Congress.*

great turnpike—from Boston through Providence and Newport and on to New York and Philadelphia—New London was the home of the U.S. Naval Office, hence the activity of war vessels and privateers, along with guests to the Shaw residence.[21]

Lucretia's congeniality also extended to those in need. She cared for the abused prisoners coming back from the floating disconsolate British gaols and garrison pens. These were the most reviled institutions of their day, reeking of filth and waste. The returning souls were often the sickest of the sick, repulsive in order, yet Lucretia Shaw did not balk. Her very last act on earth, the personal attendance to a number of indisposed prisoners, took her very life. Infected with a contagious disease, and after a short illness, she perished on December 11, 1781, at the young age of forty-four. Witnessing her compassion, and heartbroken by her loss, her husband passed on April 15, 1782, at the age of forty-seven.[22]

Mary Silliman

Born in 1736, Mary Silliman spent the early years of her life in North Stonington, located at the southeast corner of the state.[23] As the eldest daughter of the Reverend Joseph Fish, she witnessed the enrichment of education and the refinement of etiquette. Her son would later recall observing no "finer example of dignity and self-respect," her elegance welcomed by the finest social circles of the day.[24]

On November 16, 1758, at the age of twenty-two, Mary took the hand of the Reverend John Noyes, son of Reverend Joseph Noyes, pastor of the first church of New Haven. Educated in the ministry, John was as committed to his service as to Mary's attention, and the pair soon saw to a family of three sons. But John's health had been failing, and less than a decade after their marriage, he died (1767). Ever resolute, Mary then took to the upbringing of her children, whom she saw all reach adulthood, and two of the three serve as faithful ministers of the Gospel.

On May 21, 1775, Mary then took the hand of Colonel Gold Selleck Silliman, later to become a brigadier general of the Continental army. Silliman, a former prosecuting attorney, had lost his first wife, Martha Davenport, on August 1, 1774, leaving him to raise their nineteen-year-old son, William.[25] The newlyweds settled in the family home, which overlooked Long Island Sound, on an impressive perch located two miles from Fairfield and called Holland Hill.

Gold Silliman's responsibility was to oversee the vigilant defense of the state's southwestern frontier, which, because of its proximity to Long Island and New York (the city having been taken control of by the British on September 15, 1776), required the utmost in efficiency.

Managing the couple's domestic affairs, Mary guided the family—which now included five boys, a son Gold born on October 26, 1777—with a confidence and security drawn from her spirituality. It was the "love of a merciful God," she believed, that marshaled her family and kept them safe; it also protected her husband at the Battles of Long Island and White Plains, the latter of which saw a "spent ball" found conspicuously in the lining of the general's jacket.[26] It was Silliman who, along with Generals Wooster and Arnold, gave brilliant resistance to the British attempt to destroy the military stores at Danbury in 1777. So much so that Sir Henry Clinton, impressed by his enemies' fighting prowess, executed a plan for Silliman's abduction, a scheme successfully carried out on May 6, 1779.

Lying in her bed, child nestled beside her, Mary heard the enemy burst through the doors of her home at midnight. Despite her husband firing on the invaders, it was to no avail. With bayonets fixed, the British surged into the Silliman bedroom and overtook their prey. Instead of an outcry of fear, Mary remained steadfast and unimaginably composed. Led away were both her husband and son William, the latter eventually released on parole. With Fairfield now a "hotbed" of resistance, and fear of invasion a daily occurrence, Mary was forced to flee to the protection of one Eliakim Beach in Trumbull.[27] Thankfully, in May 1780, a prisoner exchange finally saw to the return of General Silliman; he would pass on July 21, 1790, at the age of fifty-eight years. Left with two sons to educate and a family of servants to provide for, Mary again turned to her faith for endearment. It would not fail her.

At the age of sixty-nine, the widow again married, becoming the spouse of Dr. John Dickenson of Middletown in 1804. When he died in 1811, Mary lived principally in Wallingford with her son Reverend Joseph Noyes (II). She died there on July 2, 1818, aged eighty-three.

Elizabeth Clarke Hull

The wife of Captain Joseph Hull III, Elizabeth Clarke Hull was also the proud mother of three sons who served in the American Revolution: Captain Joseph Hull, Colonel William Hull and Samuel Hull.

Born in Lyme on September 24, 1732, Elizabeth was the daughter of William Clarke and Hannah Peck of New Haven. Her lineage included that of William Clarke and his first wife, Sarah Wolcott, and his second wife, Hannah Griswold, who was the ancestor of Governors Matthew and Roger Griswold; her great-grandfather Thomas Clarke, by accepted tradition the mate of the *Mayflower* and for whom Clarke's Island is named; and her mother, who was a direct descendant of William Peck of New Haven.

The eldest of ten children, Elizabeth Clarke married her neighbor Captain Joseph Hull III, the son of Joseph Hull II and Sarah Hull, when she was seventeen. The couple had six sons and two daughters: Joseph (born 1750), William (born 1753), Samuel (born 1755), Elizabeth (born 1759), Isaac (born 1760), David (born 1765), Sarah (born 1769) and Levi (born 1771).[28]

For Elizabeth Clarke Hull, the years and tears of independency would forever change her life. Her husband answered the first call for troops and departed for New York. But upon his return, Captain Joseph Hull was seized by a sudden illness that took his life in September 1775. Three weeks later, the couple's youngest son, Levi, died at the age of four. Elizabeth's whole world seemed to be falling apart.

As the war opened, the eldest son, Joseph, entered the army, leaving behind three young sons of his own (the second of whom was Isaac, destined to become the famous commander of the *Constitution*) and his wife, Sarah. During the futile defense of Fort Washington, Lieutenant Hull was taken prisoner and confined for two grueling years; he was exchanged and returned in 1778.

William, a Yale graduate and classmate and friend of Nathan Hale, attended private classes at the prestigious Litchfield Law School and was later admitted to the bar (1755).[29] Selected as captain of the first company organized in Derby, William Hull marched to Cambridge, crossed the Delaware with Washington, fought at both Saratoga battles and even endured the 1777–78 winter at Valley Forge. Having one of the most illustrious careers of the conflict, William Hull would also secure the family name for posterity.

Of the others, Samuel, the third son, served to the rank of lieutenant. The fourth son, Isaac, too young for the Revolution, would later prove his loyalty in 1812.

Of the grandchildren, those of distinction included the aforementioned Isaac; Abraham Fuller Hull, the only son of William and who fell at the Battle of Lundy's Lane; and Levi Hull, aide to General William Henry Harrison. In characteristic Hull fashion, the accomplishments of their descendants would be equally as impressive.

On October 14, 1776, Elizabeth Clarke Hull, over a year of grieving now behind her, married Sergeant Joseph Tomlinson of Derby. When he passed, she wed Captain Joseph Osborne of Oxford on February 13, 1793. And Elizabeth took nuptial vows for a fourth time, to Captain James Masters of Schaghticoke, New York. At the age of ninety-four, she passed on February 11, 1826, and was laid to rest by the side of her first spouse, Joseph Hull.

CODICIL

In 1779, a valiant Judith Sargent Murray challenged the view that men had greater intellectual capacities than women. She argued that whatever differences existed between the intelligence of men and women were the result of prejudice and discrimination. This, she believed, was what prevented women from sharing the full range of male privilege and experience. Regrettably, her support for gender equality was met largely by shock and disapproval.

Tragic also has been historical accounts of this era. While women are often described by their looks and temperament (as exemplified by some direct quotations in this work), perhaps it is also time to describe them by their accomplishments—an exacting task, considering their suppression at the time.

Clearly, as we have just witnessed, women contributed a great deal—immeasurable in courage alone—to the American Revolution. And the archaic belief that women lacked the rational faculties of men was simply absurd. What women accomplished at home and on the battlefield allowed men to reach their goals more quickly and with a greater degree of efficiency. It was through the assistance of women that the Continental army was able to fully concentrate on defeating the British and acquiring our sovereignty.

We must sweep away this misconception, so grab a broom—and while you're brushing, remind yourself that there is simply not enough gratitude, even in the great state of Connecticut, to express our appreciation for the women of the American Revolution.

SECTION II
The Families

Chapter 3

THE ELLSWORTH FAMILY
OF WINDSOR

I t was, as some believe, the most critical moment in the history of the
United States, and Oliver Ellsworth was there as both witness and
participant. At a distance measured in inches (as if democracy is ever so
short a linear distance) over feet, he observed the "unshaken confidence" of
John Adams, who, after a solemn invocation, stepped down from a platform
to a table at the front of the chamber. Now positioned directly in front of
Chief Justice Ellsworth, Adams would be administered the presidential oath
of office. As instructed, John Adams repeated the words (that although not
everyone heard, most certainly felt) to confirm the successful transfer of
executive power. As functionary, Oliver Ellsworth was the very first person
to look into the eyes of the second president of the United States.

On this day, March 4, 1797, tears of sadness and joy would flow—the
weeping, heard by Ellsworth and others, had begun early in preparation
for the departure of the beloved first president and the arrival of his
successor—inside Congress Hall in Philadelphia. As the first-floor (House)
chamber filled, Ellsworth and his fellow justices mingled with bicameral
legislators, diplomats and privileged guests; the conversation was light
and the atmosphere solemn. The dignified occasion was interrupted only
by applause, including that of the chief justice. It rang out in tribute at
the sight of a serene countenance of George Washington and continued
with the arrival of the blue frock–coated Thomas Jefferson, who had been
inaugurated vice president in the upstairs room of the Senate earlier that
morning. With the appearance of Adams, even Ellsworth himself could

Portrait of Oliver Ellsworth, a drafter of the U.S. Constitution, U.S. senator from Connecticut and the third chief justice of the United Sates. *Library of Congress.*

not help but feel moved by the triumvirate that stood before him—they would never again appear on the same platform. It was a historical frame, a priceless reflection of the old ardor of the American Revolution.

A Pillar of Patriotism

Oliver Ellsworth was born on April 29, 1745, in Windsor, Connecticut, to Captain David and Jemima Ellsworth. As a youth, he was instructed by the respected educator Reverend Dr. Joseph Bellamy and prepared for his higher education. Ellsworth entered Yale College in 1762 but graduated from the College of New Jersey (now Princeton University) four years later.[30] While the father hoped the son would choose the ministry, Oliver saw it differently. Following a year of theology, he turned toward the legal field. Intense study—with the first Governor Griswold of Connecticut and later with Judge Jesse Root of Coventry—led to his bar admittance in 1771, followed by his limited practice in Windsor.

Dividing his time between woodcutting and the law was a difficult task for Oliver (his father had given him a house and farm in Wintonbury, now Bloomfield), but as his legal success grew, so, too, did his reputation. When law, and a bit of political interest, finally took precedence, he sold his farm and moved to Hartford. A political Whig, he served as a member of the General Assembly, as state attorney and as a member of the Continental Congress (1778–83). Ellsworth was also a member of the governor's council, judge of the Connecticut Superior Court (1785–89) and, most notably, a delegate to the 1787 convention that framed the federal Constitution. It would be he, along with fellow state agents, who would author the Connecticut Compromise.

Serving in the United States Senate from March 1789 until March 1796, Ellsworth was installed as chairman of the committee to organize the nation's judiciary; he would then tender his resignation to accept a judicial nomination. Oliver Ellsworth was appointed chief justice of the Supreme Court in the spring of 1796; he succeeded John Jay (Jay's replacement, John Rutledge, had been rejected by the Senate), the first chief justice. Confident, courteous and dignified, he would become a stable force (John Adams called him "the firmest pillar of Washington's whole administration") in the early works of our legal system.

Although Ellsworth would accept a European appointment (as envoy extraordinary and minister plenipotentiary to France to negotiate a treaty) in 1799, his health had begun failing. His son Oliver Jr., who had accompanied him overseas as his secretary, accepted the task of traveling home to deliver his father's resignation from the Supreme Court.

Upon Ellsworth's return in 1801, he was again elected a member of the governor's council (1802), of which he had no peer. Later, he accepted but then declined an appointment as chief justice of the Supreme Court of Connecticut (1807). He simply was in no condition to serve. Oliver Ellsworth passed on November 26, 1807.

Lost was a dignified man, referred to by Daniel Webster as "a gentleman who had left behind him, on the records of the government of his country, proofs of the clearest intelligence and of the utmost purity and integrity of character."

OF FAMILY

Abigail Wolcott had a strength and endurance all her own. Born on February 8, 1756, she was the daughter of William Wolcott, Esq., a Patriot of the Revolution, and Abigail Abbott, of South Windsor.[31] On December 10, 1772, at the age of sixteen, Abigail married Oliver Ellsworth, who was eleven years her senior. Aware of his ambition, she seemed to welcome the challenges it presented. She was, after all, a Wolcott.

References to Abigail speak of a genuine thoughtfulness and concern for others, even during an embarrassing and often-recalled encounter when she once greeted a visiting guest at the door in a working dress. When the Pennsylvania gentleman asked if Mrs. Ellsworth was at home, she replied affirmatively yet added that Mrs. Ellsworth was busy and could not see him until the afternoon. When he returned, the refined Lady Ellsworth received him in a becoming gown, powdered hair and fancy cap; the guest never realized he was speaking to the same individual.

To her husband, she was a blessing, deflecting household concerns to ensure that nothing disturbed his work. Steadfast and unwavering, Abigail displayed little anxiety even in the most difficult of times.

As parents to a family of nine, the Ellsworths instilled public morals and the value of civil service to all their children.

Abigail, or "Nabby," as she would be called, was born on August 16, 1774. As a teenager, she traveled with her father to Congress in Philadelphia in 1790 and was the delight of his eye. She would marry merchant Ezekiel Williams, of Wethersfield, on October 20, 1794. His father, by the same name, was the sheriff of Hartford County (1767–89) and, during the Revolution, served as a member of the Committee of the Pay Table and as deputy commissary general of prisoners in Connecticut. The senior Williams, who was born in

Elmwood, the historic Windsor, Connecticut home of Oliver Ellsworth. Two U.S. presidents—George Washington and John Adams—were guests of the Ellsworth family.

Lebanon to the prominent First Church minister Solomon Williams, was brother to Signer William Williams. Ezekial and Abigail Williams would have six children.

A son, Oliver (II) was born on October 22, 1776, but died on May 20, 1778. After the death of their young son, Oliver penned a beautiful letter to Abigail: "This world has now fewer charms in my eyes than it once did & I have no doubt but you can say the same. Happy for us, if it keeps a better world more constantly in view, and is a means of bringing us to those joys and rest into which I fully believe our dear departed little son is already entered."[32]

Oliver Jr. (III) was born on April 27, 1781. Upon his graduation from Yale in 1799, he accompanied his father on his mission to France. His health, like his father's, suffered from the transatlantic trip. He received an AM or Artium Magister (master's) degree in 1802, three years before his death on July 4, 1805.

Martin, born on April 17, 1783, in Windsor, married Sophia Wolcott, daughter of Senator Samuel Wolcott and Jerusha Wolcott of East Windsor.

Martin served as a major in the War of 1812. When his mother passed in 1818, he moved his family into his parents' home.[33] Martin died on November 2, 1857; his wife passed on June 8, 1870. The couple had six children.[34]

Another son, William, was born on June 25, 1785, but died on July 24 of the same year.

Frances, or "Franny," was born on August 31, 1786, and died on March 14, 1868. Franny married Judge Joseph Wood of Stamford, Connecticut, on May 10, 1809, and the couple had five children.

Delia, the youngest daughter, was born on July 23, 1789. She married the Honorable Thomas Scott Williams of Wethersfield, another son of Deacon Ezekial Williams and Prudence Stoddard, on January 7, 1812. The couple had no children. Delia would pass on June 24, 1840.

On November 10, 1791, Oliver and Abigail Ellsworth welcomed their final family members, twin boys Henry and William.

Henry graduated from Yale in 1810 and married Nancy Allen Goodrich three years later, on June 22. The couple had three children before she died on January 14, 1847. As an active lawyer, businessman and farming enthusiast, "Harry," as he was also known, then met and married Marietta Mariana Bartlett, who died on April 17, 1856. Henry then took Catherine Smith as his final spouse. He passed on December 27, 1858.

William also attended Yale and graduated in 1811. "Billy," as his father called him, married Emily Scholten Webster (1790–1861), daughter of Noah Webster Jr. and Rebecca Greenleaf, on September 14, 1813. A professor at Trinity College in Hartford for most of his life, William also represented Connecticut in the U.S. House of Representatives (1829–34) and served as governor of the state between 1838 and 1842. William and Emily had six children, five of whom lived to adulthood. Governor Ellsworth died on January 15, 1868.

THE HAWLEYS, ABIGAIL AND A HOME IN WINDSOR

The Hawley family, Joseph Hawley (1603–1690) being the first in name to make the transatlantic voyage, was prominent in the early history of the colony of Connecticut. Settling in Stratford, he would draw wealth from his landholdings and businesses.[35] Abigail Wolcott Ellsworth's parents were

William Wolcott and Abigail Adams, the former the son of a father of the same name and Abiah Hawley.[36]

With such an impressive lineage, one would expect much from Abigail, and that is precisely what she delivered. Early in her marriage, she tended to the needs of the home while Oliver built his law practice. The Ellsworths were a strong couple, Oliver's aspirations matched only by Abigail's fortitude. It was her forbearance and awareness that provided a constant in the lives of their children. She saw to the boys' need of higher education yet did not limit the girls' horizon; no better exemplified than her acceptance of Nabby's travels with her father.[37] The deaths of her infant children, while never forgotten, seemed to be eased a bit by the birth of the twins.

Solace for Abigail could be found at Elmwood, the couple's Windsor home. Built by Samuel Denslow in the same year as the birth of Oliver Jr., it was appropriately named for the thirteen elm trees (representing the original colonies) that were planted on the premises.[38] The home rested on family property and was a two-story, wooden-framed building peaked with a cedar shake roof and clapboard exterior walls. A two-story addition, constructed by Thomas Heyden, was added in 1788, allowing for a first-floor drawing room and an additional upstairs bedroom. Elmwood, which exists today, has the distinction of being visited by two sitting presidents, George Washington on October 21, 1789, and John Adams on October 3, 1799.[39] Washington, on his way to Boston to meet with John Hancock, the governor of Massachusetts, enjoyed his visit and was said to have sang with the children. Bound for Trenton, where he would arrive the following day, Adams enjoyed the visit but was coming down with one of his now-infamous colds.

One can only wonder the compelling conversations that took place between not only the couple but also their Elmwood guests. Oliver's political positions, particularly during the time he served on the committee that prepared the first draft of the Constitution, were passionate and no doubt a target for criticism.[40] However, if Abigail had to deal with any political repercussions while living in Windsor, which is almost certain, she appears to have kept them confidential. At age sixty-three, she died on August 4, 1818.

A Calvinist with Federalist interests, Oliver was born into a New Light family in the aftermath of the Great Awakening. Guided by the doctrines of the New Divinity theology that dominated New England, he conducted his affairs with pride while raising and supporting his family. With religion as a core value, his mind was clear and his vision unclouded.

The First Church is the oldest Congregational church in Connecticut and, some believe, the fourth-oldest Congregational church in the world. The Ellsworth family is buried behind the place of worship.

Respecting order, and abhorring chaos, Oliver's depth and deference for liberty can be understood from his writings: "Liberty is a word which, according as it is used, comprehends the most good and the most evil of any in the world. Justly understood it is sacred next to those which

The Ellsworth grave marker inside the Palisado Cemetery in Windsor.

we appropriate in divine adoration; but in the mouths of some it means anything, which enervate a necessary government; excite a jealousy of the rulers who are our own choice, and keep society in confusion for want of a power sufficiently concentered to promote good."[41]

Chapter 4

THE HALE FAMILY OF COVENTRY

Everyone was running from the fire. From burning buildings came people screaming and coughing, looking for refuge of any kind. But there was none to be found. The falling debris and cracking timbers created the horrific sound of death and destruction. The city of New York was ablaze, and there was little, if anything, anyone could do about it.

Only a portion of the resident British troops were assisting, as their commanding officer, General Howe, was in fear that the blaze was a prelude to an enemy attack. By noon the following day, September 21, 1776, nearly a quarter of the city, or five hundred homes, had been reduced to ashes. Over one hundred suspects—incendiaries, at least to British eyes, no doubt under the command of Washington himself—were rounded up and questioned, but fruitlessly. All the prisoners were eventually released due to the lack of evidence.

Captain Nathan Hale, on a covert spy mission, witnessed the devastation and was "apprehended"—so some believe—as part of the muster. Regardless of the circumstances of his seizure (others believing his mission was nearly complete and that he was taken while trying to gain the attention of a nearby sloop), the Coventry, Connecticut native, who had taken his orders from none other than the distinguished Thomas Knowlton, had been captured. During Hale's interrogation, he admitted to Sir William Howe that he was a spy. Incriminating evidence found in his possession supported the claim. Without a trial, he was ordered hanged for his actions.

Raised on rich Connecticut farmland, Nathan Hale came from good stock, that of Richard Hale and Elizabeth Strong.[42] He was a Yale graduate,

The statue of Nathan Hale, by artist Bela Lyon Pratt, honors the heroism of the Yale College graduate and stands before the hall where he once roomed.

a teacher and profoundly loyal. The handsome twenty-one-year-old served with distinction at battles such as the Siege of Boston, and his military prowess had earned him a place among "Knowlton's Rangers." But none of his aptitude had prepared him for the peril he was about to face. His secret mission—doomed from the start, or so believed by his closest of friends, including Captain William Hull—had landed the volunteer in the clutches of the enemy.

On September 22, 1776, Nathan Hale was sent to the gallows in an artillery park near the Beekman house, near the East River. Under a flag of truce, Captain John Montresor would later inform Captain Hull of the fate of his friend. Hull echoed what he had heard, that Hale's last words were "I only regret that I have but one life to lose for my country." An alteration of the then-famous quote from Addison's Cato, the line would reverberate for centuries and send Hale into the pantheon of American heroes.

PARENTAL LOVE AND GUIDANCE

Nathan Hale's father, Deacon Richard Hale (1717–1802), was the grandson of Reverend John Hale (1636–1700), the first minister at the First Parish Church in Beverly, Massachusetts. A contemporary of the Reverend Samuel Parris of Salem Village, John Hale supported the prosecution of witches during the delusion of 1692; however, when his second wife, Sarah, was accused of witchcraft, Nathan's great-grandfather withdrew his position and renounced the legal proceedings. The words "hardworking," "strong willed" and "trustworthy" described Nathan's father. He ran a regimented household overseen by his strict patriarchal hand. Home, farm, church, school, chores and play were the priorities of the day. Nathan's father and grandfather Strong, both of whom were deacons of the church, combined with Reverend Dr. Joseph Huntington, their pastor, to provide the youth more than his fair share of New England Congregationalism.

When American author Washington Irving quipped, "The tie which links mother and child is of such pure an immaculate strength as to be never violated," he could have easily been speaking to the bond between Nathan Hale and his mother, Elizabeth Strong. Born sickly on June 6, 1755, Nathan needed to be nurtured. Although it was a task assumed by the entire family, it was always under the watchful eye of Elizabeth.

In 1767, Nathan's mother and baby sister, Susanna, died within months of each other.[43] The unthinkable tragedy, as one could only imagine, had a profound effect on the family. For maternal guidance, the children then turned to their mother's mother. "Forget not frequently to visit and strongly to represent my duty to our good grandmother Strong. Has she not repeatedly favored us with her tender, most important advice? The natural tie is sufficient, but increased by so much goodness, our gratitude cannot be too sensible," Nathan would pen to his brother Enoch.[44]

Following a period of mourning, Deacon Richard Hale married Mrs. Abigail Adams, widow of Captain Samuel Adams of nearby Canterbury, on June 13, 1769.[45] Both families were far from strangers, as Abigail's daughter Sarah courted and eventually married John Hale, Nathan's elder brother. Another Adams daughter, Alice, would join the household at the insistence of Deacon Hale. Quickly catching the fancy of Nathan and Enoch (certainly an incentive for both to visit more frequently from college), Alice, too, would have made a welcome daughter-in-law, but such was not to be.[46] Family integration can be as dynamic as it is complex.

OF RICHARD HALE AND ELIZABETH STRONG

Richard and Elizabeth Hale were married in May 1746 and had twelve children. Of the first three sons, Samuel Hale (1747–1824) lived in Coventry and had no children. Major John Hale (1748–1802) married Sarah Adams, daughter of his father's second spouse, on December 19, 1771. The couple had no children and settled in Coventry.[47] Lieutenant Joseph Hale (1750–1784)[48] served in the distinguished regiments of both Thomas Knowlton and Charles Webb. He married Rebeckah Harris, daughter of Judge Harris, on October 21, 1777. The couple lived in Coventry and had four children.[49]

Elizabeth (II) (1751–1813), the eldest daughter of Deacon Richard Hale, married army surgeon Dr. Samuel Rose on December 30, 1773. The couple had three children: Captain Joseph Rose, Nathan Hale Rose and Fanny Rose.[50]

Of the next four boys, Enoch (1753–1837) entered Yale with his brother Nathan in 1769 and graduated in 1773. Studying theology, he was ordained on September 28, 1779, and accepted a ministry in Westhampton,

The Nathan Hale Homestead in Coventry. The current house, constructed in 1776, was the second dwelling built on the property.

Massachusetts. Enoch married Octavia Throop, daughter of Reverend Throop of Bozrah, Connecticut, on September 30, 1781. The couple had a family of eight children: Sally, Nathan (II), Melissa, Octavia, Enoch (II), Richard (III), Betsey and Sybella. Nathan (1755–1776), the American hero, followed. Richard (II) (1757–1793), who married Mary Wright of Coventry on March 16, 1786, was the next boy. Richard died during a trip (an excursion designed to reinvigorate his health) to St. Eustatia in the West Indies. The couple had three children. The last of these three, Billy (Billey) (1759–1785), married Hannah Barker of Franklin. The couple had one son, who died early in life.[51]

Twin boys were born to the Hales next. David (1761–1822), whose twin brother, Jonathan (1761), died as an infant, graduated from Yale in 1785 and became a minister in Lisbon, Connecticut. Marrying Lydia Austin, daughter of Samuel Austin of New Haven, on May 19, 1790, he later moved to Coventry and became the deacon of the church (1806). The couple had one child, David (II).[52]

The last two of the Hale children were girls. Joanna (1764–1838), the second daughter of Deacon Hale, married Dr. Nathan Howard, of Coventry, on January 22, 1784. The couple had nine children. And the last to be born was Susanna (1766).[53]

Not to Be Confused

Enoch's eldest son, Nathan (II), was born on August 16, 1784, and graduated from Williams College in 1804. He then settled in Boston, practiced law and founded the *Boston Daily Advertiser* (serving as both editor and publisher for a half century) in 1813. Nathan married Sarah Preston Everett (sister of Edward Everett), daughter of Reverend Oliver Everett, on September 5, 1816. The couple would have eleven children (the fourth of whom was the noted orator Reverend Edward Everett Hale), of whom four died in childhood.

Edward Everett Hale

At the young age of two, Edward (whose father was the nephew of Nathan Hale) attended Miss Susan Whitney's school with his siblings. Charting an educational path that would impress the most gifted scholar, he entered Boston Latin at age nine, matriculated to Harvard at age thirteen and graduated in 1839. Edward then wrote and taught while studying for the ministry. Licensed to preach in 1842, he held positions at the Congregationalist Church of the Unity in Worcester, Massachusetts, from 1846 to 1856 and then moved to South Congregational Church in Boston, where he was minister until 1899.

In 1852, Edward married Emily Baldwin Perkins of Hartford, Connecticut. She was the daughter of Thomas Clap Perkins and Mary Foote Beecher and niece of Catherine Beecher, Henry Ward Beecher, Harriet Beecher Stowe and Isabella Beecher Hooker.

A talented wordsmith, Edward wrote on a variety of topics—everything from the abolition of slavery and religious tolerance to education reform and social reform—for the two magazines he founded, *Old and New* (1870–

75) and *Lend a Hand* (1886–97), and for a number of fiction and nonfiction book publishers. Hale's most noted work was the short story "A Man without a Country," first published in *The Atlantic* in December 1863.[54]

Edward Everett and Emily (Perkins) Hale had one daughter and eight sons, three of whom (Alexander, Charles Alexander and Henry Kidder) died in childhood.[55] Ellen Day Hale (1854–1939) did not marry and became a successful artist; Arthur Hale (1859–1939) worked for the Pennsylvania Railroad Company; Philip Leslie Hale (1865–1931) was an artist, writer, art historian and art teacher; Edward Everett Hale Jr. (1863–1932), or "Jack," was an author; Herbert Dudley Hale (1866–1908) was an architect; and Robert Beverly Hale (1869–1895) was a writer.

EDWARD EVERETT AND THE "OTHER" GETTYSBURG ADDRESS

As a member of the U.S. House of Representatives (1825–35), a United States Senator (1853–54), the governor of Massachusetts (1836–40), the secretary of state (1852–53, under Fillmore) and president at Harvard University, Edward Everett, the uncle of Edward Everett Hale, was the featured speaker at the dedication of the Gettysburg Cemetery on November 19, 1863. Unfortunately, his two-hour speech was overshadowed by the "dedicatory remarks" of Abraham Lincoln.

In a bit of irony, Everett—whose sister married the nephew of Nathan Hale—was appointed minister to Great Britain by President William Henry Harrison. Also raising $70,000 for the Mount Vernon Ladies Association, which sought to preserve the home of George Washington, Everett was a vice presidential candidate on the 1860 Constitutional Union ticket. It is his marriage to Charlotte Gray Brooks that links the Hales to the family of John Adams.[56]

Naturally, Nathan, as the martyr spy of the American Revolution, attracts most of the family attention. However, in fairness, it is the Hale lineage that symbolizes love of country.

Chapter 5

THE HUMPHREYS FAMILY OF DERBY

The few surviving actors from the stage of the Revolutionary war will become daily more and more scarce. We leave this scene not for a tittering generation we wish to push us from it, but for those who, we hope, will act their parts much better in peaceful improvements. Long may you enjoy the fruits of our labours!
—David Humphreys, address to the Agricultural Society in Connecticut, September 12, 1816[57]

Far more than a gifted orator and poet, David Humphreys was also a soldier, diplomat and industrialist. As an accomplished man of the American Revolution, his prolific writings were not only a reflection of history but also empirical evidence of its consequences. As for his military aptitude, particularly his role as aide-de-camp to General George Washington, Humphreys performed admirably, later also proving himself a talented foreign minister (first in Lisbon and then in Madrid) and even a visionary of the American textile trade. Drawing international attention for his "restless energy and versatility," Humphreys is painted as a man of innumerable talents whose zest for life seemed boundless.[58]

A statue of David Humphreys adorns the exterior of the Hartford State Capitol.

OF THE FATHER

Daniel Humphrey, David's father, was born to Deacon John Humphrey and his wife, Sarah Mills, in 1707. He was the youngest of five children: John, Hannah, Benjah, Michael and Daniel. As if it were predestined, Daniel became the beloved pastor of "the first Church of Christ." From the day of his settlement on March 6, 1734, until his death on September 2, 1787, he had the complete confidence of the people of Derby. In colonial Connecticut, the ministers who served in the Congregational or Presbyterian churches had their rights confirmed by law.[59] This position, as one might expect, was one of profound respect.

As a graduate of Yale (class of 1732), Daniel possessed formidable leadership and arbitration skills. When the conscience of New England split into two camps—those who shunned change, or the "Old Lights," saw themselves differently from the "New Lights," or those who welcomed new ideas—he believed himself the ideal arbiter. This division, responsible for the political factionalism in Connecticut, was a sensitive shift in ideology, and it required an authority of Humphrey's deftness.[60]

Sarah Riggs, the daughter of Captain John and Elizabeth (Tomlinson) Riggs, was born in Derby on December 17, 1711. She married John Bowers on November 22, 1732, and the couple had two children, Nathaniel and Sarah. Sadly, in 1738, Sarah Riggs Bowers would experience the death of her children and spouse before year's end. She would then marry Reverend Daniel Humphrey on April 18 of the following year.

Descendants of Sergeant Edward Riggs, the man who valiantly assisted Colonel John Mason in destroying the Pequot Fort in Groton, the family was no stranger to adversity. The ancestry had claimed their stake in 1654, when Derby was still known by its Indian name of Paugassett. But Sarah was far more than just a survivor; she was a woman of charm and elegance—a true "Lady."[61] Her aristocratic deportment shined brilliantly through her passion for the arts and literature. It is doubtless that her love of painting and poetry (an alluring avocation) played a role in capturing her husband's heart. Sarah would pass on July 29, 1787, separated from Daniel by only five weeks.

THE FAMILY

The Reverend Daniel and Sarah Humphrey would have five children (four sons and a daughter). Daniel (II) (1740–1827) married Mary King, John (1744–1832) married Rachel Durand, Elijah (1746–1785) married Anna Mansfield and Sarah (1748–1827) married Reverend Samuel Mills, who passed in 1814. Widowed, she then married Chipman Swift in 1819. Finally, David was born on July 10, 1752.[62]

Most ministers typically had large families and supplemented their salary by farming on their "settlement land." It was an early lifestyle conducive to providing their sons with a college education and their daughters a befitting (as were the times) home life.

Eldest son Daniel graduated from Yale College in 1757 at the age of seventeen. Admitted to the bar in New Haven in 1762, he was a Sandemanian (a Christian sect spread by Robert Sandeman into England and America) and reportedly never stayed in the courtroom while the minister delivered the opening prayer. After the Revolution, he settled in Portsmouth, New Hampshire, where, in 1804, he became the U.S. district attorney. As a scholar, he enjoyed the beauty of language, even becoming proficient in Italian after the age of seventy. He also wrote on the topic of religion. His pamphlet, *The Bible Needs No Apology*, which he penned in 1796, even found its way into the hands of Thomas Jefferson in 1801.[63]

Second son John and his wife, Rachel, became the quintessential farming family. Living on his father's homestead for a time, the family eventually settled in a home north of, and adjoining, the old Episcopal cemetery. Successful husbandry, no doubt through the efforts of a large family combined with that of hired hands, yielded the family many benefits, including the option of education. The Humphreys had eight children.[64] It was said that "a four pail iron kettle filled with corned beef, pork, potatoes and turnips was boiled every day for forty years, Sundays excepted," inside the Humphreys' home.[65]

One could only imagine the tavern gossip that surrounded the son of the Congregational minister marrying the daughter of the town's Episcopal vicar, but such was indeed the case when Elijah Humphrey joined hands with Anna Mansfield. The couple would have five children: Anna (1775–1850), Sally (1777–1865), Elijah (1779–1834), Betsey (1781–1864) and David (1784–1809). As a major in the Connecticut militia during the Revolutionary War, Elijah is said to have had three horses shot from under him. Unfortunately for everyone, especially the young children, Elijah's life would be lost at sea.

Following the death of Reverend Samuel Mills, Sarah took the hand of Chipman Swift, Esq. He, too, had lost a spouse, Mary Laine. The couple met when Chipman moved from Wilmington, Vermont, to Derby to live with his son, the Reverend Zephaniah Swift. Sarah, as one might presume, reflected much of her mother's social gifts.

DAVID HUMPHREYS

Common has been the practice of linking Yale's Revolutionary poets, the Connecticut Wits: John Trumbull, the noted artist; Joel Barlow, the ardent Jeffersonian; Timothy Dwight, whose family developed a long association with Yale College; physician Dr. Lemuel Hopkins; author Richard Alsop; and David Humphreys.[66] Upon his academy entrance, the latter developed a strong bond with two in particular, Dwight and Trumbull.

A member of the class of 1771, Humphreys, like many Yale graduates, was expected to teach. And he did, in the beautiful Connecticut town of Wethersfield. As the principal of the New School on Main Street, it has been said he came at the perfect time. The handsome young Humphreys was tall and muscular, with wavy hair that topped a jovial countenance. His departure in 1773, the year before he completed his master's degree, left a void that would be filled by another Yale graduate, Benjamin Tallmadge. He, too, would chart a course of immortality.

While tutoring in New York from 1773 until 1776, Humphreys, too, heard the call to arms. From the militia, he rose quickly through the ranks, becoming an aide to General Israel Putnam (in 1778), General Nathaniel Greene (in 1780) and General George Washington (from June 1780 to the end of the hostilities) and attaining the rank of lieutenant colonel.

WASHINGTON AND HUMPHREYS

The fellowship between Washington and Humphreys was incontestable to the point of being envied by others who had also served the general; aide and artist John Trumbull would quip that Humphreys was "belov'd of Washington."[67]

The general's trust was forged—following Danbury and Sag Harbor—by Humphreys's military acumen, even if his undertakings weren't always successful. On Christmas Night 1780, the general approved a secret mission to be led by his talented lieutenant colonel. A small band of brave men was to quietly row down the Hudson River, land at the home of Sir Henry Clinton, demobilize the enemy, restrain their prize and hustle him back up the river. But the covert operation was abandoned due to high winds.

Following the Battle of Yorktown, the general honored him with the task of presenting twenty-four captured British flags to Congress. In turn, the legislative body presented Humphreys with a commemorative sword. Commemoration for both he and his mentor also came courtesy of Trumbull. Immortalized in *Washington Resigning His Commission*—a canvas filled with artistic liberties yet flattering to most attendees—Humphreys, standing immediately behind the general, appears as gallant and nearly as tall as the future first president.

Washington also coveted the young man's talent for composition. As a capable wordsmith, the poet would craft a bulk of the leader's later remarks, including his first inaugural address—although the Constitution said nothing about such reflections, Washington felt it a necessity. For seventy-three pages, the two would battle over words and phrases, the end result being a curious defense of Washington's decisions.[68]

Agreeing to Humphreys's persistent request to pen a biography, Washington extended his own home to the writer (this, knowing that objectivity would be impossible for the author) during the summer of 1786. Later, the general would position the work—valued now for Washington's assessment of the French and Indian War—more of a history of the Revolution than a personal reflection.[69]

Later, Humphreys again returned to Washington's side, attending to the newly elected president in his New York home on 3 Cherry Street (1789).

DIPLOMAT, MANUFACTURER AND POET

In 1784, Congress appointed Humphreys secretary of the committee designated to negotiate commercial treaties in Europe. For two years, he handled himself masterfully with his now-trademark precision. Returning home in 1786, and following his time at Mount Vernon, he was selected to serve in the Connecticut legislature.

Humphreys's international dealings continued when he was named the first U.S. minister to Portugal in 1791. Five years later, he was made minister to Spain, where he developed an interest in textile production, particularly the efficient breeding of sheep for wool production. His eventual introduction of the Merino breed into his home state improved not only Connecticut's production but also the manufacture of quality fleece in America.

As a poet, Humphreys seemed to shine from his first verse, "An Address to the Armies of the United States of America," written in 1782. The inspirational piece became a patriotic call to duty. "A Poem on the Happiness of America," "A Poem on the Future Glory of the United States," "A Poem on the Industry of the United States" and "A Poem on the Love of Country" fell into a similar vein. As a writer, he was never short of praise for those he admired, as evidenced by "A Poem on the Death of Washington" and "An Essay on the Life of the Honourable Major-General Israel Putnam."

In 1797, David Humphreys married Ann Bulkeley, the daughter of an Englishman.[70] Although the couple would have no children, they shared a love for the arts. No doubt political dynamics also played into conversation, as Portugal's new ruler, Queen Maria I, harbored tremendous animosity (not to mention a bit of mental instability) toward her predecessor Joseph I. Like many Europeans, she was also uncertain as to just where America fit into the political horizon—insights Humphreys detailed in voluminous accounts of the period.

One of Jefferson's first acts as president was to remove as many of the Federalist officeholders as he could. Notwithstanding his faithfulness, ability and proficiency, Humphreys could not escape his displacement. The fatigue and inconvenience suffered by Ann during the voyage home prevented her husband from making a customary journey to Washington to pay his respects to the new president.[71] Upon arriving in his native land, a preoccupied Humphreys ceased a bulk of his literary activities.

Humphreys's postwar accolades included honors from Brown University and Dartmouth College, as well as a membership in the British Royal

David Humphreys, the subject of this gravesite plaque, is buried at Grove Street Cemetery in New Haven.

Society. He was even commissioned a brigadier general in command of the "Veteran Volunteers" (exempt from military duty) in response to the War of 1812. During this time, he also served his town in the state's House of Representatives for five sessions from 1812 until 1814.

On February 21, 1818, David Humphreys passed in his room at Butler's Tavern while convalescing in New Haven. After her husband's death, Ann Humphreys continued to live in their home on Mount Vernon Street in Boston. On December 31, 1829, she married Count Etienne Cajetan de Walewski at her home. The countess died in Paris on March 2, 1832.

OF SOUND CONSCIENCE

Inherently, the American Revolution put the sword of freedom into the hands of two of the sons of Daniel and Sarah Humphrey, Elijah and David.

Driven by their spirituality and devoted to their country, community and kin, both (aware of the risk and understanding of the repercussions) served proudly and with distinction.

> *'Tis like a moon-light vision's airy shade,*
> *A bubble driving down the deep beneath*
> *Then, ere the bubble burst, the vision fade,*
> *Dissolv'd in air this evanescent breath!*
> *Let man, not mortal, learn true life begins at death.*
> *—David Humphreys, portion of sonnet "On Life"*[72]

Chapter 6

THE HUNTINGTON FAMILY OF
WINDSOR AND NORWICH

News of the exploits at Fort Ticonderoga and Crown Point reached the Connecticut General Assembly in May, soon after it opened its regular 1775 session. Evoking not only cheers—many of the Tories having been weeded out following the recent election and replaced by a solid Whig legislature—but also actions, legislators quickly moved, as in previous periods of war, to create an emergency committee, the Council of Safety. It would be the duty of this elite group to handle the day-to-day events while the legislature was not in session. Headed by Governor Trumbull and Deputy Griswold, the committee included surnames like Dyer, Elderkin, Huntington, Wales, West and Williams. Although the personnel would fluctuate over the course of the war, this small group of men remained active and engaged. During over one thousand meetings, many held inside the "War Office" in Lebanon, the issues of the day were debated and state resources maneuvered to meet the cause of freedom. Three of those selected men—Jabez, Benjamin and Samuel—shared the surname of Huntington.

JABEZ HUNTINGTON (1719–1786) AND FAMILY

Among the most distinguished members of the Huntington extended family were Jabez and his sons: Jedidiah, Andrew and Ebenezer. As an active and very successful West India trader, Jabez was not only a forceful family patriarch but also a leader in both his community and the state legislature. His diligent labor as an original member of the Council of Safety ran from 1775 until 1779.

In September 1776, Jabez, alongside David Wooster, was promoted to major general of the militia. And it was he who took charge of the entire Connecticut force following Wooster's tragic death at Danbury.

Born on August 7, 1719, Jabez Huntington graduated from Yale in 1741. That same year, he also married Elizabeth Backus (1721–1745), his second cousin.[73] The couple had two children: Jedidiah, born on August 4, 1743, and Andrew, born on June 21, 1745, just days before his mother's death (July 1). In 1746, Jabez then married Hannah Williams (1726–1807). The couple had six children: Joshua, Hannah, Ebenezer, Elizabeth, Mary and Zachariah.[74]

In 1779, Jabez suffered a stroke—perhaps, as many believe, a result from the tremendous stress created by the war—and remained in poor health until he died in Norwich on October 5, 1786.

JEDIDIAH HUNTINGTON (1743–1818)

A 1763 graduate of Harvard College, Jedidiah received his master's degree from Yale College seven years later. A noted member of the Sons of Liberty, he joined the army at Cambridge on April 26, 1775, just a week after the Battle of Lexington. The regiment he commanded was detailed for the occupation of Dorchester Heights. Following the evacuation of Boston by the British, Huntington marched with the army to New York. By 1777, his service—having held the rank of colonel with the Eighth Connecticut Regiment (1775), the Seventeenth Regiment of Connecticut Infantry (1776) and the First Connecticut Regiment (1777)—had earned him the complete credence of General George Washington. He was commissioned to brigadier general in the Continental army and, by war's end, brevetted major general.

Jedidiah married Faith Trumbull, daughter of Jonathan Trumbull, on May 1, 1766. The couple had a son, Jabez (II). Upon her passing, he would marry Anne Moore, daughter of a New York businessman, and the couple would have seven children.[75]

The General Jedidiah Huntington House in the town of Norwich, Connecticut, was built in the Georgian architectural style in 1765.

As a respected intellectual, Huntington was a member of the court-martial that tried General Charles Lee for misconduct at the Battle of Monmouth, and he sat on the court of inquiry assigned the case of British major John Andre. He also proudly played a role in the formation of the Society of the Cincinnati. Huntington's retirement came with the disbandment of the army in 1783, and he died on September 25, 1818.

ANDREW HUNTINGTON (1745–1824)

A successful paper manufacturer at the Falls of Norwich, Andrew was a commissary during the Revolution. He married twice, first to Lucy Coit (1746–1776) in 1766 and then to Hannah Phelps (1760–1838) in 1777.

EBENEZER HUNTINGTON (1754–1834)

At the outbreak of the war, Ebenezer Huntington left his studies at Yale (where he eventually would graduate) to join the army. Serving first at Lexington, before being appointed to first lieutenant in a Connecticut regiment led by Colonel Samuel Wyllys, his prestigious service (he is depicted as one of the officers of General Washington's army in Trumbull's masterful *Surrender of Lord Cornwallis*) lasted until the end of the war.

Married twice, Ebenezer had one son, Alfred Isham Huntington, by his first wife, Sarah Isham (1771–1793), of Colchester, and had a much larger family by his second wife, Lucretia Mary McClellan (1773–1819), of Woodstock. Their children included Wolcott, Louisa Mary, George Washington, Nancy, Walter, Sarah, Elizabeth and Maria.

As a Federalist to the Eleventh Congress (1810–11), Ebenezer Huntington was also elected to the Fifteenth Congress. He died in Norwich on June 17, 1834.

BENJAMIN HUNTINGTON (1736–1800) AND FAMILY

A Yale graduate (1761) and accomplished Norwich attorney, Benjamin Huntington began serving in the Connecticut House of Representatives in 1771. This, along with his role on the Council of Safety, was the perfect prelude to his appointment (on the recommendation of George Washington) to the 1778 Provincial Congress at New Haven. He would also serve as a member of the Continental Congress (1780, 1782, 1783 and 1788), the Connecticut Council of Assistants and the State Senate.

With the origination of the new government, Huntington was chosen—as a Pro-Administration Party candidate—to represent his home state in the First Congress of the United States, from March 4, 1789, to March 3, 1791. Later, he was elected the first mayor of Norwich (1784–96).

Born on April 19, 1736, Benjamin was the only child of Daniel Huntington and his second wife, Rachel (Wolcott) Huntington; grandson of Deacon Simon and Sarah (Clark) Huntington; and great-grandson of immigrants Simon and Margaret (Beret) Huntington, first in America. He was also the first cousin twice removed of Ebenezer Huntington.

At age twenty-nine, Benjamin married Anne Huntington of Windham, Connecticut, on May 5, 1765. They were second cousins, once removed.[76] The couple had eight children: Henry (1766–1846), a 1783 Dartmouth graduate who abandoned law in favor of the mercantilism he found in upstate New York and married Catherine M. Havens; Gurdon (1768–1840), who first Married Susannah Tracy (1770–1793) and later Anna Perkins (1768–1802), became a successful carriage maker and later removed to Rome, New York; George (1770–1842), who was the first to establish the Huntington stronghold in upstate New York and also was considered "the patriarch of the village" (Fort Stanwix)[77]; Lucy (born 1773), who married Dr. Matthew Brown and resided first in Rome, New York, and then Rochester; Anne "Nancy" (1775–1842), who never married; Benjamin (born 1777), father of the noted portrait painter of the same name; Rachel (born 1779), who married William Gedney Tracy; and Daniel (born 1781). Benjamin Huntington died in Rome, New York, on October 16, 1800.

SAMUEL HUNTINGTON (1731–96) AND FAMILY

By the time Samuel Huntington found himself inside Trumbull's War Office, he had already handled the roles of king's attorney, tax collector, town-meeting moderator and justice of the peace (Norwich) and had been appointed to the Superior Court (1773). He was a self-made man, whose determination and fairness had evoked the respect of many, including that of his first cousin once removed, Benjamin Huntington.

Samuel, born on July 3, 1731, was the second son of Nathaniel Huntington (1691–1767) and his wife, Mehetabel Thurston Huntington (1700–1781). As a Scotland, Connecticut youth, Samuel is believed to have apprenticed as a cooper while assisting on the family farm. At age twenty-two, Samuel, who had had his fill of farming, turned to law. Five years later, he was admitted to the bar and moved to Norwich (1754) to practice.

In 1761, he married Martha Devotion (1738–1794), daughter of his local pastor and mentor, Reverend Ebenezer Devotion.[78] While the couple would have no children of their own, they welcomed those of friends and relatives. When Martha's sister Hannah—who had married Samuel's brother, the Reverend Joseph Huntington (1735–1794)—died in 1771, two of their three children came to live in a new Huntington household. Uncle

---

Samuel, who became the adoptive father of both children, had a profound impact on young Samuel H. Huntington (1765–1817), who would become the governor of Ohio (1808–10), while Aunt Martha delighted in Frances, the other child, who married Reverend Edward Door Griffin, at one time president of Williams College. Although this branch of the family might not have been the most traditional, the love provided by both Samuel and Martha was as conspicuous as it was enriching.

Elected to Connecticut's Upper House of Assembly in 1776, Samuel was also selected a delegate to the Continental Congress. As president of the congress, during the important adoption of the Articles of Confederation, he would serve two terms. Huntington's peers considered him perfect for the role, as he was a man of sound and firm judgment yet mild mannered. "Tho' not a man of many words or very shining abilities," he was efficient in his duties and, in the words of Benjamin Rush, "wholly free from State prejudice."[79] When he was elected lieutenant governor of Connecticut, a homesick Samuel welcomed the call.[80] In 1786, he was elected governor, and he was reelected every term until his death on January 5, 1796.

It was Huntington's state leadership, however, that is most often overlooked. Connecticut, like other states, faced sizable financial stress, a condition the governor felt could be tempered (he set forth an agenda to encourage business development through pecuniary incentives) by sound economic considerations. He also catered to the needs of war veterans by establishing procedures to handle injury and property claims; created a permanent school fund for the state, and with it the establishment of banks in support for continued education; and, in perhaps his most courageous move, barred state residents from participating in the slave trade.

Assuredly, when Samuel Huntington put ink to paper and signed both the Declaration of Independence and the Articles of Confederation, he guaranteed his immortality. But there was far more to this Connecticut gentleman.

AS PRESIDENT OF THE UNITED STATES

Elected to the largely ceremonial position of president of the congress, in September 1779, Samuel Huntington might have been in the right place at the right time. In March 1781, the Articles of Confederation became operative as the first constitution of a new nation. Since Samuel Huntington's

Jurist, diplomat and Patriot Samuel Huntington was the third cousin of Samuel Adams. *Library of Congress.*

term didn't end until July 1781, he was the country's first president of "The United States in Congress Assembled."

And his presidential links go a bit further. Huntington was the third cousin of "The Psalm Singer" Samuel Adams (1722–1803). Samuel, as second cousin of President Johns Adams (1735–1826), was also a second cousin once removed of President John Quincy Adams (1767–1848).

ROOTS

Simon Huntington (1583–1633), who immigrated in 1633 with his wife, Margaret Beret Barrett (1595–1666), is the common ancestor of all those previously mentioned.[81] The couple had five children. Although Simon died of small pox en route to Boston, his wife carried on and settled in Roxbury, Massachusetts. Margaret later married widower Thomas Stoughton, of nearby Dorchester, and the couple moved to the settlement of Windsor, Connecticut.

THE GRANT-HUNTINGTON CONNECTION

Having been united more than once through marriage, the Grant and Huntington families have a unique—and albeit a bit hard to follow, due to the duplication of names—bond. Matthew Grant (1601–1681) married Susanna Rockwell, the widow of William Rockwell. Her second daughter, Ruth Rockwell, married Christopher Huntington, the great-grandfather of Anne Huntington, the spouse of Benjamin Huntington (1736–1800).

Martha Huntington, a great-granddaughter of Christopher Huntington, married Noah Grant, a great-grandson of Matthew. A second (Captain) Noah Grant came from this marriage. Now, Captain Grant's third son, also named Noah (1748–1819), lived in Coventry, Connecticut, and had a son named Jesse Root Grant (1794–1873), who was the father of President Ulysses S. Grant.[82]

As a family with unique ties to the United States presidency, the Huntingtons have few rivals.[83]

Chapter 7
THE JOHNSON FAMILY
OF STRATFORD

Dr. Johnson is a character much celebrated for his legal knowledge; he is said to be one of the first classics in America, and certainly possess a very strong and enlighten understanding.
—*William Pierce, member of the United States Constitutional Convention of 1787*

Born on October 7, 1727, in Stratford, Connecticut, William Samuel Johnson was the son of well-known Anglican clergyman-philosopher Reverend Doctor Samuel Johnson and Charity Floyd Nicoll. With a father who was also the founder and first president of King's College (later Columbia University), Samuel's adolescence was filled with indoctrination. His graduation from Yale came in 1744 and was followed by his master of arts degree three years later. The latter Yale diploma was accompanied by an honorary master's from Harvard.

As might be supposed, the father saw his reflection in the son and assumed a path to the ministry, but young Samuel saw a contrasting image and turned to a career in law. Self-taught, he was admitted to the bar and began practicing in Stratford. As a gifted orator, his mesmerizing voice—not to mention a proficiency in law that earned him the Connecticut moniker "Father of the Bar"—was so rich in tone that it could almost instantly transfix an audience. Soon his legal proficiency extended beyond state borders, adding to his growing wealth and reputation.

William Samuel Johnson was the son of well-known Anglican clergyman-philosopher Reverend Doctor Samuel Johnson (pictured here) and Charity Floyd Nicoll. *Library of Congress.*

FAMILY MATTERS

William Samuel Johnson married the wealthy Anne Beach (1729–1796), daughter of William Beach (1694–1751) and Sarah Hull, on November 5, 1749.[84] The couple is believed to have had five daughters and six sons. Those who lived to adulthood included Charity (1750–1777), who married Reverend Ebenezer Kneeland; Sarah (1754–1762); Gloriana

74

The Honorable Gulian Crommelin Verplanck, son of Daniel Crommelin Verplanck and Elizabeth Johnson and grandson of William Samuel Johnson. *Library of Congress.*

Ann (1757–1785), who married Roger Alden; Mary (1759–1783); Samuel William (1761–1846), who married Susan Pierrepont Edwards;[85] Elizabeth (1763–1789), who married New York State representative Daniel Crommelin Verplanck;[86] and Robert (1766–1806), who married Catherine Anne Bayard.[87]

Four years after the passing of Anne, William Samuel Johnson wed Mary Brewster Beach, of Kent, Connecticut, the widow of his first wife's brother. The couple would have no children and settle in Stratford.

A BRITISH BUFFER

Johnson's civic responsibilities saw him as a militia officer before turning to state government. Elected first to the Lower House of the Colonial Assembly in 1761 and 1765, followed by the Upper House of the Colonial Assembly in 1766 and 1771–75, his conflicting loyalties led to his refusal to participate in the First Continental Congress (1774). While he believed British policy imprudent, he did not radically oppose it—he was not a member of the extremist Whig faction. Johnson's association with both the mother country and the Anglican Church was amiable, and he intended, as difficult as it might sound, to keep it that way.[88] Acting as Connecticut's agent in Britain during the years 1767–71, Johnson tried his best to diffuse the hostility. An independent America, Johnson thought, could quickly factionalize and become susceptible to foreign invasion. This was a concern shared among scholars, but in varying degrees of proclamation.[89] Forever judicious, and always erring on the side of caution, Johnson abhorred violence, and ironically, his pro-peace activities (he was an Anglican in Calvinist Congregational Connecticut) never seriously affected his prestige.

Acting as a judge of the Connecticut colonial supreme court (1772–74) before the hostilities, Johnson was soon called to action. In April 1775, he was sent as a state emissary to speak to British general Thomas Gage about ending the bloodshed. But Gage, more concerned with preserving his reputation than dealing with the pleas of a colonist, was not in a position of compromise. Johnson was unsuccessful. As the radical elements ascended in state government, the experienced legislator gradually fell out of favor.

Later, for agreeing to make peace (on behalf of his hometown of Stratford) with a former friend of his, British general William Tryon, Johnson was arrested. When cries of treason erupted, he was jailed briefly before his appearance in front of the Council of Safety. After taking an oath of fidelity to the state, Johnson was permitted to return to home.

POSTWAR EFFORTS

As the memory of armed conflict faded, Johnson reentered politics. Serving diligently in the Continental Congress (1785–87), his persuasive manner was welcomed at the Constitutional Convention. Along with his fellow Connecticut agents, Roger Sherman and Oliver Ellsworth, Johnson struck a welcomed balance with the passage of the Connecticut Compromise. He also signed the U.S. Constitution.

The new government also saw Johnson's service, as a senator from Connecticut (1789–91). His influence assisted in the passage of the Judiciary Act of 1789, a critical law that established the details of the federal judiciary system.

In 1790, when the government relocated from New York to Philadelphia, the requirements of service—not to mention serving also as the first president of Columbia College (1787–1800)—began to take a toll on the leader. In 1791, he resigned to devote all his efforts to education. On November 14, 1819, while in his hometown of Stratford, William Samuel Johnson died.

By remaining in a neutral position between two protagonists, both of whom he respected, Johnson stands in history as an ideal example of just how to avoid extremism.

Chapter 8

The Parsons Family of Lyme and Middletown

I too...
Shall tell from whom I learned the martial art,
With what high chiefs I played my part,
With Parsons first, whose eye with piercing ken
Reads through their hearts, the character of men.
—*David Humphreys, portion of "The Happiness of America"*[90]

To be held with such reverence in the eyes of a Patriot like David Humphreys speaks volumes for the ethos of General Samuel Holden Parsons. As "solider, scholar, judge," in the words of George Frisbie Hoar, the talented commander was "one of the strongest arms on which [General George] Washington leaned," both in Boston, at Breed's Hill, and in Brooklyn, at Battle Hill.[91]

Born on May 14, 1737, in Lyme, Connecticut, Parsons would distinguish himself early in the war before shifting his endeavors to recruiting, training and local defense efforts. Tragically drowning on November 17, 1789, during a canoeing accident, death came early to Parsons, but not before he created a lasting persona.

General Samuel Holden Parsons was a shoulder on which General George Washington (pictured here) rested his confidence. *Library of Congress.*

SPRINGFIELD ROOTS

Deacon Benjamin Parsons, an early settler of Springfield, Massachusetts, married Sarah Vore in 1653. The couple established a large family, Ebenezer being the sixth of nine children.

Ebenezer Parsons, the grandfather of General Samuel Holden Parsons, was born on November 17, 1668, in Springfield, Massachusetts. He married

Margaret Marshfield, daughter of Samuel Marshfield and Katherine Chapin, and had a large family. Their youngest son, Jonathan Parsons, the general's father, was born on November 30, 1705, in West Springfield. Graduating from Yale in 1729, Jonathan was ordained pastor of the Congregational church in Lyme on March 17, 1731.

At the young age of twenty-five, Jonathan, having studied theology under Yale president Reverend Elisha Williams and, later, with Reverend Jonathan Edwards, was quick to impress his congregation. Among his flock was a "bright, witty and vivacious" girl, not quite sixteen years of age, and her name was Phebe Griswold. As the daughter of Judge John Griswold, one of the wealthiest and most respected men in town, she was established and dignified. Parsons was immediately drawn to the young woman, and the two were married.[92]

This period also witnessed Jonathan's friendship with George Whitefield, a popular English Anglican preacher. As a founder of Methodism and of the evangelical movement, Whitefield was spreading the word of the Great Awakening throughout the colonies. It was so profound a view that it caused Parsons's resignation in 1745. He was then installed as a pastor at a new church in Newburyport, Massachusetts. When he died on July 19, 1776, he was buried beneath his pulpit alongside George Whitefield and Joseph Prince in the crypt of Old South Presbyterian Church.

GRISWOLDS AND WOLCOTTS

It has been said that to understand the colonial politics of Connecticut is to acknowledge the life and family of Ursula (Wolcott) Griswold. Her father, Roger Wolcott, was colonial governor of Connecticut (1750–54); her brother, Oliver Wolcott Sr., a Signer, among other things; and her husband (Matthew), son (Roger Griswold), nephew and four cousins all governors of Connecticut.[93] Ursula married her cousin Matthew Griswold IV, brother of Phebe Parsons. It was the second unification of both families.

Ursula was an aunt of Oliver Wolcott Jr., who besides being governor was also the U.S. secretary of the treasury and uncle of General Samuel Holden Parsons and Senator James Hillhouse (1796–1810).[94]

MATTHEW GRISWOLD IV (UNCLE)

Matthew Griswold IV was born on March 25, 1714, inside Black Hall, the family estate, in Lyme. Receiving minimal formal education, he decided to study law in his mid-twenties and was admitted to the New London Bar in 1742. The young man's assiduous, adamant and assertive behavior would not go unnoticed. On November 10, 1743, Matthew married Ursula Wolcott, and the couple had seven children.

Ascending rapidly through public office, Griswold was quick to impress. He was captain of the Train Band (local militia) in 1739 and king's attorney (New London) from 1743 until 1776. His additional service included: deputy for the Connecticut General Assembly (1748, 1751–59) and Council of Assistants (1759–69), judge on the Superior Court (1765–69), chief justice of the Connecticut Superior Court (1769–84) and deputy governor (under Jonathan Trumbull) for the Colony of Connecticut (1769–84). When Governor Trumbull decided not to run for reelection in 1784, Griswold came forward. Although he did not receive a majority of the votes in the regular election (a situation that had also affected his predecessor), the General Assembly chose him for the position. Reelected as governor in 1785, he was succeeded by Samuel Huntington the following year.

After forty years of marriage, Ursula passed in April 1788. Matthew died over a decade later, on April 28, 1799, and is buried alongside Ursula in Old Lyme's Duck River Burying Ground.

THE AMERICAN REVOLUTION

Following his graduation from Harvard, in 1756, Samuel Holden Parsons studied law with his uncle Matthew Griswold in Lyme, Connecticut. Admitted to the bar in 1759, he then began his own practice. Two years later, he married Mehitabel (also spelled Mehetable) Mather (1743–1802), a great-great-great-granddaughter of Puritan cleric Reverend Richard Mather. In 1762, at the age of twenty-five, Parsons was then elected a member of the General Assembly of the Colony of Connecticut. He would be continually reelected for a dozen years until his removal to New London.

A plaque inside the Lebanon War Office salutes the distinguished officers of the Continental army, including Parsons, who met there during the conflict.

As an active member of New London's Committee of Correspondence, Parsons became an outspoken voice of resistance. Five years after having been appointed major of the Fourteenth Connecticut Militia Regiment (1770), he found himself commissioned a colonel of the Sixth Connecticut Regiment and ordered to Boston. While there, the British troops twice assaulted Parsons's troops, who were dug in on the high ground at Breed's Hill, and both times were repelled.

TICONDEROGA

On April 26, 1775, Samuel Parsons, who was returning to Hartford from Massachusetts following the Lexington alarm (April 19, 1775), met a company of volunteers and their captain, Benedict Arnold, on their way to Cambridge. According to a letter of the same date, from Parsons to his classmate Joseph Trumbull, Arnold "gave him an account of the state of

Parsons, who was returning to Hartford following the Lexington alarm, met a company of volunteers under the command of Benedict Arnold (pictured here). *Library of Congress.*

Ticonderoga, and that a great number of brass cannon were there." While surprising the fort would have certainly been offered as a consideration, just who deserves the credit for the idea remains debatable. Four days later, Arnold was commissioned colonel and authorized by the Massachusetts Committee to raise troops for the capture of the fortress. As for Parsons, upon his arrival in Hartford, he called on Colonel Samuel Wyllys and Silas Deane and, according to the same letter, "first undertook and projected taking the Fort &c, and with the assistance of other persons procured money men & c." On April 28, Parsons, along with Wyllys and Deane, elicited the assistance of Thomas Mumford and Adam Babcock and together gave their own "promissory receipts." The money was then entrusted to riders, who would find their way north to offer a mission to Colonel Ethan Allen and his Green Mountain Boys.

Battle of Long Island

In August 1776, having been appointed brigadier general in the Continental army, Parsons was ordered to defend the port city of New York, then limited to the southern end of Manhattan Island. Washington had begun moving troops to Brooklyn (Brookland) in early May, and Parsons was part of that first line of resistance. But the failure at both Brooklyn (the westernmost county on Long Island) and Kips Bay (a neighborhood in the city borough of Manhattan) would not augment the careers of any of those involved.[95] Following the enigma, Parsons's brigade was assigned to Israel Putnam's division, north of the city, where they would battle unsuccessfully at White Plains on October 28, 1776. Later, in 1777, he returned to Connecticut.[96]

Often overlooked in the military career of Samuel Holden Parsons were his successful recruitment efforts and able defense of Connecticut towns; selection of the first submersible pilot, Ezra Lee; command of West Point (winter of 1777–78) and Putnam's Division (December 1779); and participation on the board of officers that tried British major John Andre.

On May 17, 1782, General Parsons wrote to General Washington and announced his retirement from the army due to "extreme ill-health," a condition that included suffering from malaria that he had contracted in the Highlands. At forty-five years of age, and having served continuously since he entered the army on April 26, 1775, Parsons had served with distinction.

The Children of Samuel Holden Parsons

"With Parsons, as with Washington, it was Independence or nothing. He had sacrificed the interests of his family, his property and his health to the Cause, and his determined, uncompromising spirit would consent to nothing short of unconditional surrender on the part of the British Crown," according to author Charles S. Hall.[97] His role left him little choice but to turn his large family over to the capable hands of Mehitable.

As for the Boys

William (1762–1802) was a fifer in the Sixth Connecticut Regiment from May until December 1775. He served as a midshipman aboard the Continental frigate *Warren* during the Revolution, when he was taken prisoner by the British during the disastrous Penobscot Expedition (summer 1779). He escaped his captors in 1780. Ironically, in 1781, he was captured and again escaped. William Parsons and Esther Phillips, of Middletown, were married on February 9, 1784, and eventually settled in Bangor, Maine.[98]

Thomas (1767–1778), of which little is known, was born in Lyme and died in Middletown, according to family records.

Enoch (1769–1846) eventually accompanied his father to Ohio, where he served as registrar and clerk of probate. Returning to Connecticut after his father's death, he served as high sheriff of Middlesex County for twenty-eight years and as president of the Middletown branch of the Bank of the United States from 1818 until 1824. Enoch married Mary Wyley Sullivan, of Philadelphia, on May 19, 1795. The couple had three children: Mary Sullivan, Enoch Thomas and Samuel Holden (III). Enoch's son, Samuel Holden Parsons (III) (1800–1871), was a lawyer and banker in Middletown. After the death of his first wife, Enoch Parsons married Mrs. Sarah Rosecrans, of Middletown. The couple had one child, Henry Ethelbert.

Samuel Holden Parsons (II) (1777–1811) became a merchant active in West Indies trade. He married Esther Sage, of Middletown, in February 1803. The couple is believed to have had only one child, Mary Anne. Samuel Parsons died in the West Indies in March 1811.

As for the Girls

Lucia Parsons (1764–1825) married Stephen Titus Hosmer (1763–1834), of Middletown. Mr. Hosmer became chief justice of Connecticut. The couple enjoyed a very large family: Titus Samuel, who died at sea; Lucia Parsons (II); Harriet Lydia; Lucia Parsons (III); Sarah Mehitabel Hosmer (1793–1834), who married Major Andre Andrews III (1792–1834), second mayor of Buffalo (1833); Elizabeth Lord; Mary Whiting; and, finally, Oliver Ellsworth, named for Chief Justice Oliver Ellsworth of the U.S. Supreme Court, with whom his father studied.

Mehitable Parsons (1772–1825) married William Brenton Hall, a Middletown physician, on March 6, 1796. The couple had three children: Mehitable Parsons Hall, who died as an infant; William Brenton Hall (1798–1824); and Samuel Holden Parsons Hall (1804–1877).

Phebe Parsons (1775–1797) married Samuel Tifflin on July 30, 1797. The couple had a daughter, Eliza.

Margaret Parsons (Hubbard Lathrop) (1785–1853) married Stephen Hubbard of Middletown on February 10, 1807. The couple settled in Champion, New York, and had two children: Mary Sullivan, who married the Honorable Joel Turrill, a member of Congress and consul at the Sandwich Islands during Polk's administration, and William Hubbard. Stephen Hubbard died on March 27, 1812, and Margaret later married Alfred Lathrop. Their children included Stephen Hubbard, Samuel Parsons, George Alfred, Eliza Storrs, Enoch Thomas and Frederick.

CIVILIAN LIFE

In the summer of 1782, Samuel Holden Parsons returned to Connecticut. While his primary goal was to replace his depleted finances, he could not turn his back on his other interests. He quickly garnered a seat in the legislature, became involved in the Connecticut branch of the Society of the Cincinnati and even picked up a congressional appointment on the western frontier. Parsons also became a director of the Ohio Land Company, a program that enabled ex-Revolutionary officers to trade their pay certificates for Ohio lands.

In March 1788, Parsons and his son headed west for the Northwest Territory to survey the Ohio Company's lands while also purchasing choice parcels for his family. By summer, it became clear—as indicated by his correspondence—that his health was suffering. On August 4, 1789, Samuel wrote to Enoch Parsons, "It, therefore, becomes my duty to commend to your care your mother and the family, to whom you must become a father and protector." He later added, "Preserve a life of strict honor and honesty in all your dealings and pursue a steady course of industry, and with all remember that the religion of the Scriptures is a serious truth."[99] Parsons drowned a few months later. His body was reportedly discovered the following spring and buried in an unmarked grave along the Beaver River in Pennsylvania.

LOYALTY AND RECRIMINATION

The idea of inalienable allegiance to any Prince or State, is an idea to me inadmissible; and I cannot see but that our ancestors when they first landed in America were as independent of the Crown or King of Great Britain as if they never had been his subjects.
—Samuel Holden Parsons to Samuel Adams

In 1888, nearly a century after Parsons's death, George B. Loring authored *A Vindication of General Samuel Holden Parsons,* against the then-recent charge of treasonable correspondence during the Revolutionary War. Inside the thirty-eight-page book, he pens a lengthy letter to Mrs. Martha J. Lamb, editor of the *Magazine of American History* (and who had referenced letters from double-agent William Heron to Sir Henry Clinton that seriously injured Parsons's reputation) with hopes of vindicating the general.[100]

A peculiar letter had been discovered in the manuscript volume of Sir Henry Clinton's original record of daily intelligence. It revealed that Parsons was in secret communication with the British officer through one William Heron, a spy and member of the Connecticut legislature; that Heron was acting as an intermediary; and that Parsons knew that his letters to Heron were being forwarded to the enemy's headquarters.[101]

Knowledgeable of many of the covert channels of intelligence, Heron, whose indicting and brilliantly crafted correspondence with the enemy began in February 1778, denounced other clandestine sources and even referenced Washington's intelligence lattice, later known as the "Culper Ring."

McCurdy offers a few points, arising chiefly from the letters alone, and Charles S. Hall concludes, "A man with treason in his heart does not breath this freedom [referring to examples he has given in his letter]... The tongue of slander may revile him, but none but the clearest and most incontrovertible evidence can weigh much against him in any candid and unprejudiced mind."

That such a preposterous conversation was being conducted nearly at the centennial of Parsons's death was considered a disconcertion. Yet it still remains an interminable debate.

Chapter 9

THE PETERS FAMILY OF HEBRON

*The best excuse that can be made for him is that he was a victim of
pseudomania; that his abhorrence of truth was in fact a disease, and that he was
not morally responsible for its outbreak.*
—*Doctor J. Hammond Trumbull*[102]

SAMUEL PETERS VERSUS JONATHAN TRUMBULL

The ominous clouds of conflict, precipitated either by colonist or Tory, arose gradually over the rolling hills of eastern Connecticut as public proclamations and even threats became more frequent. Even though the May 1774 session of the General Assembly had declared allegiance to George III, it also denied, in unequivocal terms, the British Parliament's right to levy taxes; the only lawful representatives of the freemen of this colony, they believed, were those persons elected to serve in the General Assembly. Conflict, be it the form of proclamation or tax, was unavoidable.

Samuel Andrew Peters, born in Hebron, Connecticut, on November 20, 1735, was the tenth child and sixth son of John Peters (1695–1754) and Mary Marks (1698–1784).[103] In 1757, after graduating from Yale College, he traveled to England, where he was ordained in the Church of England.

Three years later, Peters returned to Hebron as a commissioned missionary and became rector of St. Peter's Church.

Peters was a man of conviction and strongly opposed the prevailing sentiments. It was he, by his own telling, that convinced the people of Hebron (during a town meeting at the request of Governor Trumbull) to vote a majority against sending aid or supplies to Boston during the enforcement of the Port Bill—a result of the Destruction of the Tea. According to Peters, every clergyman in the colony was required to read a circular to their respective congregations "and to urge the selectmen to warn town meetings to appoint a general contribution for the support of the poor people in Boston, shut up to starve by General Gage and Admiral Graves."[104] He then affirmed, "Hartford, following Hebron, unanimously negatived to vote for a general collection," which put a stop to the town meetings in Connecticut, to the disappointment and mortification of Governor Trumbull, who laid the blame on the influence of Dr. Peters, the Episcopal clergyman of these two towns.[105]

Of course, this did not sit well with the opposition—referred to as the "Windham mobs"—who decided to pay two visits to Reverend Peters.

On August 14, 1774, a committee of ten requested and received papers from Peters with the written assurance that he had not corresponded or would continue to correspond with his English friends regarding his state of affairs. The group then left Peters without injury.[106]

On September 6, 1774, the meeting was not so friendly. The Bolton Committee of Correspondence had caused Peters's "Resolves of the Town of Hebron" to be published in the *New London Gazette*. Such a proclamation could not be tolerated. An argument ensued, near riotous by some accounts, including the claim of a discharged firearm. Notwithstanding the provocation, damages included "the breaking of one window sash, one punch bowl and glass, and the tearing of Mr. Peters' gown and shirt."[107] Upon signing a document, or as some believe an intervention by Reverend Benjamin Pomeroy, the mob released the reverend.

However, Peters's account—which included "three bold troopers" from Hebron who threatened death to the rabble mob commander—varied and even included a claim that the governor's son David was a part of the angry horde.[108] The incensed reverend, who visited the governor the following day, soon decided to flee to Boston and then on to England in October 1774.

In a statement regarding the incident, Governor Trumbull remarked in the closing paragraph:

Mr. Peters' religious sentiments, his being a member of the Church of England and a clergyman, were not the reasons of these transactions. Some men who were present were of the same denomination, and dissatisfied with him as well as the others. Had he been of any other denomination in religious sentiments, his treatment would doubtless have been the same.[109]

Later, Peters, now living in London, wrote and published under a pseudonym his controversial *General History of Connecticut* (1781). Critical and ambiguous, the work was an attempt to explicate his position before he and his family returned to the United States (1805).[110]

FAMILY MATTERS

Reverend Samuel Andrew Peters and his first wife, Hannah Owen (1739–1765), married on February 14, 1760; they had one daughter survive adulthood, Hannah Delvena (1762–1845). After his first wife's death, Peters married Abigail Gilbert (1752–1769) on June 25, 1769, who died soon thereafter. He then married a third wife, Mary Birdseye (1750–1774), in April 1773, and they had one son, William Birdseye Peters (1774–1822), before her death. Reverend Samuel Andrew Peters died in poverty on April 19, 1826.

WILLIAM BIRDSEYE PETERS

The only child of the Hebron Church of England minister and Mary Birdseye, William Birdseye Peters was born on June 5, 1774. With his mother dying only days after his birth and his father forced to flee the country, the youth turned to his maternal grandparents in Stratford, Connecticut. Living with the Birdseye family served him well, as William was strong-willed, articulate and scholarly—studying under both the local Congregational and Episcopal ministries. Joining his father in London (1789), he traveled Europe and matriculated into Trinity College, Oxford, on October 12, 1792. William studied law until his health took a turn for the worse, at which point he was sent to convalesce at the home of his half-sister in Canada. Hannah Peters had married William Jarvis, secretary and registrar of Upper Canada, and the couple was living in Newark (Niagara-on-the-Lake), a town located in Southern Ontario, across the Niagara River from Youngstown, New York.

Upon his recovery, William would not return to England to complete his education but instead opt to reconnect with his friends and relatives who were living in Connecticut. It would only be upon Hannah's urging that he found himself back in Canada, this time with his bride, Patty, the niece of William Jarvis.[111]

Appointed (by his father's friend, Lieutenant Governor John Graves Simcoe) as assistant secretary and registrar of the province, William practiced law and was commissioned in the Queen's Rangers. When Simcoe left, however, problems began to occur. From being unable to pursue law because he was an army officer to repercussions with the Jarvis family, William's employment options ran out.

In 1798, Peters applied for a commission in the American army. But soon, he felt differently and moved to York (Toronto), where he reported for duty in the British army. As one can imagine, this change of allegiance, or treason, depending on your perspective, caused all sorts of problems—issues that would forever plague Peters.

Yet the attorney persevered. Peters served with the Rangers until his regiment disbanded (1802), practiced law and then moved to New York to start a dry goods business. Despite the transition, he just could not escape his misfortune. From bankruptcy to additional charges of providing information to the enemy, every step forward, such as his legal defense during the "Bloody Assize," led to a step back.[112] William Peters died of yellow fever on June 4, 1822, in Mobile, Alabama.

JOHN SAMUEL PETERS

The fifth child of Bemslee (the youngest brother of Samuel Peters) and Ann Shipman Peters, John was born in Hebron on September 21, 1772.[113] His hardworking demeanor was complemented by his love for education—this despite being one of the few Connecticut governors who never graduated college. Peters soon developed an interest in medicine, and his passion,

The ornate grave marker of Governor John S. Peters states, "In his public and private life he was universally respected."

combined with diligent study and the guidance of established physicians, proved fruitful with his own Hebron practice.

As physician, he extended his profession to the militia at Fort Groton, served as president of the Connecticut Medical Society and advocated improved education. While his predominant interest was medicine, it surprised few when he sought public office. It was, as he thought, a pathway to reach his goals. Peters served as a member of the Connecticut House of Representatives (1810, 1816, 1817, 1824), clerk of the Connecticut House of Representatives (1825), delegate to the State Constitutional Convention (1818) and in the Connecticut Senate (1818–22). Then, in 1827, he became lieutenant governor of Connecticut.

When Governor Tomlinson resigned in March 1831 to become a U.S. senator, Peters was entrusted with his duties. Reelected in 1832, Governor Peters fought hard for his agenda but was often circumvented by his adversaries. His term is often associated with transportation improvements, specifically that of the railroads. Despite the fact that Peters garnered more reelection votes at the polls, the Democratically controlled General Assembly opted for Henry Edwards as the new governor.[114] The last state head to serve under the banner of the old (National) Republican Party, Peters returned home to Hebron, where he would pass on March 30, 1858.

Another nephew, John Thompson Peters (1764–1834), the son of Jonathan, the eleventh child of John and Mary Peters, served as justice of the Supreme Court of Connecticut (1818–34).[115] John married Mrs. Elizabeth Farnham Caulkins, and the couple had five children.

OF SACRIFICE AND SERVICE:
CESAR AND LOWIS PETERS

Reverend Samuel Peters's controversial departure affected many, from his congregation to members of his own family, the latter of which faced not only the humiliation of the event but serious financial consequences as well. In 1787, while living in England, Samuel Peters had little choice but to arrange for the disposal of his assets in America. This involved that of his slaves, including Cesar and Lowis Peters (slave families took the last name of their owners) and their eight children. The family had been left behind by Samuel Peters to care for his home and property.

The Peters House, purchased by the Town of Hebron in 2004, was recently added to the Connecticut Freedom Trail.

This unimaginable circumstance was compounded by the forcible apprehension of the family by a slave trader. Boarded on wagons, some with hands tied, the slaves were transported to Norwich to be loaded aboard a ship bound for South Carolina.[116]

Mortified by the news of the demeaning abduction of their neighbors, Hebron residents immediately responded. A small group concocted a creative scheme to retrieve their friends: they had a false arrest warrant issued. Convinced that the scheme just might work, they rode off toward Norwich. Upon finding the slaver, and presenting the warrant, the Peters family was released.[117]

The Peters family then returned to Hebron to fulfill a term of servitude before applying for emancipation from the Connecticut General Assembly. Convincing testimony resulted in Cesar and Lowis, along with their eight children, being declared emancipated from slavery and forever free.

For the decades that followed, the family remained an active and spirited part of the community.

Chapter 10

THE PIERCE FAMILY
OF LITCHFIELD

This feminine invasion of the home of law and jurisprudence is but a symbol of woman's entrance into the fields, not only of law, but of science and politics and all departments of the world's activities.
—Mrs. George Maynard Minor, president general of the National Society of the Daughters of the American Revolution[118]

And what a residency it would become. While any hamlet would be proud to have a story as awe-inspiring as the Litchfield Law School—a pioneering institution that transcended all rivals and provided the finest legal education of the day—associated with its community, the thought of having two such innovative educational disciplines would be inconceivable to most. Yet as law educator Tapping Reeve charted the course of his selectmen (students being transformed into judges, statesman and eminent jurists, all in hopes that they would go forth and shape a new nation desperate for strong leadership) on South Street, a pioneer of women's education, Sarah Pierce, was breaking new ground across town at her Female Academy.

A portrait miniature
of Sarah Pierce.
*Litchfield Historical
Society, Litchfield,
Connecticut [#1941-
02-2].*

FAMILY MATTERS

Sarah Pierce, born in Litchfield, Connecticut, on June 26, 1767, was the youngest of the seven children of John Pierce and Mary (Paterson).[119] Sources list the children as follows: John (1752–1788), who married Ann Bard; Mary (born 1754), who married into the Strong family; Betsy (information unknown); Anne (1758–1802); Susan (1762–1830), who married James Brace; Ruth (1764–1860), who married Thomas O'Hara Croswell; and finally Sarah.[120]

Following the death of Mary Pierce (1731–1770), when Sarah was just three, John Pierce (1730–1783) married Mary Goodman (1744–1803), and the couple had four children: James (1773–1775); Timothy (1775–1801), who became a doctor; James (1779–1846); and Mary (1780–1863).[121]

Much is said of the second Mrs. Pierce, a forceful woman who intended to stand in the shadow of no man.[122] Her presence once graced a committee of women who appealed to the Litchfield school board for a girls' curriculum equal to that of the boys'. Suffice it to say that if Sarah needed inspiration or guidance, she didn't have far to look.

At the death of her father, when Sarah was fourteen, the Pierce family responsibilities fell to her elder brother Colonel John Pierce, paymaster in the Continental army. From his letters, it is known that he handled the task admirably and welcomed the opportunity to advise his brothers and sisters. And it was he who would send Mary and Sarah expressly to New York to enhance their educational skills, perhaps even with the intent that they might one day become instructors.

THE LITCHFIELD FEMALE ACADEMY (1792–1833)

In 1792, with only one pupil in her dining room, educator Sarah Pierce charted a course toward immortality. Incorporated as the Litchfield Female Academy, the institution would transform the lives of between 1,500 and 3,000 young ladies over the next forty years, all under the watchful eye of Miss Pierce.[123]

And it seemed only natural that Litchfield, a town renowned for its culture and instruction, should be its home. By the turn of the century, the town had become a popular destination on the great inland route from Boston to New York, as well as from Hartford to West Point. As the stage lines bustled, the hamlet grew (Litchfield ranked fourth in population in the state, according to the 1820 census), surpassed by only New Haven, Hartford and Middletown. This continued until the 1840s, when the building of railroads broke up the stage routes and left some towns, such as Litchfield, somewhat less accessible.

In 1798, the school had grown to such importance that a separate building was desired. Catharine Beecher, daughter of the Reverend Dr. Lyman Beecher, recalled that "her school house was a small building of only one room; probably not exceeding 30 feet by 70 feet, with small closets on each end, one large enough to hold a piano, and the other used for bonnets and

Left: Erected by the DAR, this marker commemorates the site of Sarah Pierce's School for Instruction of Females (1792–1833).

Opposite: The Hartford home of Harriet Beecher Stowe (1811–1896), the sister of Catherine Beecher and Henry Ward Beecher. *Library of Congress.*

over garments. The plainest pine desks, long plank benches, a small table and an elevated teacher's chair constituted the whole furniture." She would later recall, "She [Miss Pierce] was sole teacher, aided occasionally by her sister in certain classes, and by her brother-in-law in penmanship."[124]

English classics, forever a favorite of Miss Pierce, also became popular with her students. The girls loved listening to her quotations, often long passages of poetry selected to inspire the youth. Of her classes, Catharine Beecher remembered, "At the time the 'higher branches' had not entered female schools. Map-drawing, painting, embroidery and the piano were the accomplishments sought, and history was the only study added to geography, grammar and arithmetic." Pierce, in stark contrast to "Dame Schools," didn't just teach girls the "ornamental" skills of the day but taught "male" academic subjects. As the school term closed, it became customary

to produce a dramatic exhibition, complete with custom sets and costuming. Miss Pierce, never short of ideas, even penned a few shows of her own.

Since there was no boarding school, a few of Miss Pierce's students boarded with her—this after 1803, when the construction of her home was complete. The rest of her scholars, similar to those of the law school, boarded with different families throughout town.

School, unlike today, consisted of a "winter term" and a "summer term," separated by three to four weeks' recess in spring and fall. The terms were governed by strict rules reviewed weekly by instructors. Naturally, the male law students of the town called on the fine young women of the academy. But understanding that it would be a disgrace to be shut out of the institution, the young men conducted themselves with the utmost care.

With four to five instructors, the academy grew to have one of the largest staffs of any private school of the day. (Yale College had only five professors and six tutors in 1812, and most comparable boarding schools had one headmaster and only two or three instructors.)

By 1827, the school had again outgrown its walls. A larger building was erected on the same lot, with funds secured by the institute's incorporation. John Pierce Brace—Sarah Pierce's nephew and the man whom she had sent to Williams College explicitly for math and science instruction so that he could return to tutor these subjects—became the director. This allowed Sarah time to focus on her foremost interest, history. The first board of ten trustees—nothing short of impressive—was also selected. It included Seth P. Beers, John P. Brace, William Buel, James Gould, Jabez Huntington, John R. Landon, Phineas Miner, Daniel Sheldon, Truman Smith and Frederick Wolcott. When Sarah Pierce finally retired, it was one of her own pupils, Miss Henrietta Jones, who succeeded her.

In 1852, at the age of eighty-four, Sarah Pierce died.[125] Over its forty-one-year history, from 1792 through 1833, the Litchfield Female Academy attracted students from fifteen states and territories, including Canada, Ireland and the West Indies. Of the students who shined, and there were many, perhaps Catharine and Harriet Beecher are quoted most. In 1823, Catharine went on to found the Hartford Female Seminary. She was far more vocal than Sarah Pierce, proclaiming in 1829 that a teacher's work was more critical to society than that of a lawyer or doctor. Her sister, Harriet Beecher Stowe, would gain recognition through her work *Uncle Tom's Cabin* (1852), a vicious indictment of the institution of slavery both for its brutality and, more importantly, its violent disruption of domestic relations.

COLONEL JOHN PIERCE

John Pierce married Ann Bard of New York, daughter of Dr. Samuel Bard, physician to General George Washington. Pierce entered the army on May 31, 1775, and was made assistant paymaster to the Continental army less than a year later. On January 17, 1781, he was promoted to paymaster general with the rank of colonel. Serving thirteen years in the paymaster's department of the army, he was a responsible and capable officer. Pierce also belonged to the Order of the Cincinnati and was a friend of General Washington.

Sarah Pierce was said to have been a small person, "of a cheerful, lively temperament, a bright eye, and a face expressive of the most active benevolence."[126] As an academic visionary, she was mindful of ambition but not limited by it. Dreams, as she saw them, were not size dependent.

Chapter 11

THE PUTNAM FAMILY
OF BROOKLYN

*Passenger, if thou art a soldier, drop a tear over the dust of a Hero, who ever attentive
to the lives and happiness of his men dared to lead where any dared to follow.*
*—monument inscription to Israel Putnam, Esq., senior major general in the
Army of the United States of America*

At fifty-seven years of age, Israel Putnam, a military veteran whose name
alone could strike fear in the heart of any adversary, was appointed
a major general in the Continental army. Of medium height and stocky
build, his prominent gray locks now flowed across a broad countenance
marked by deep battle scars. As a leader, Putnam's bravery had never been
disputed, nor had his self-confidence; his legendary exploits as a wilderness
combatant against both wolves and Indians now preceded him. And he still
commanded the respect of both the newest recruits and the most trusted
officers, including his commander, General George Washington.

Having served as a lieutenant in the Connecticut militia during the
French and Indian War and as a member of Rogers' Rangers (this unit, led
by New Hampshire officer Robert Rogers, was an independent adoption of
the British army, a precursor of modern special operations forces), Putnam
had survived an enemy capture where he was nearly burned alive and
led his regiments to victory at Fort Carillon (later Ticonderoga) in 1759
and Montreal the following year. And if that wasn't enough, "Old Put"
survived a 1762 shipwreck during the bloody British expedition against
Havana, Cuba. Following his engagement at Pontiac's siege of Detroit,

The cemetery at the (Old) Trinity Episcopal Church in Brooklyn includes many members of the Putnam family. *Library of Congress.*

this war-weary Indian fighter, battered but not defeated, returned to his Connecticut home.[127]

Putnam, who was opposed to British taxation and far from silent about the matter, was soon elected to the Connecticut General Assembly (1766 and 1767)—this while making time to found the state chapter of the Sons of Liberty. On April 20, 1775, while plowing a field on his farm, Putnam received news of an outbreak of open-armed conflict. "To arms! To arms! The first blood has been shed at Lexington!" was the call of the rider on horseback. And to arms it was. In a tale that confirmed his legendary status—carved into the capitol façade in Hartford is the image of Putnam, working in his field, turning his head over his left shoulder in response to the rider's news—he dropped his plow in favor of an eight-hour, one-hundred-mile patriotic ride to Cambridge, where he would offer his military service.[128]

In June 1775, Putnam distinguished himself at the Battle of Bunker Hill, his effective strategy earning him command of the American forces in New York the following year.[129]

However, from this point forward, his service would be questioned—first in August 1776, when he unsuccessfully commanded his divisions in Brooklyn at the Battle of Long Island, and again in May 1777, with his failed defense of the Hudson highlands, which included Forts Montgomery and Clinton. His capitulation to the enemy raised concerns regarding his ability. Putnam's weakness as a tactician had emerged: the logistics involved in directing a large inexperienced force seemed to overwhelm him. Washington was also not impressed by the speed in which his orders were being executed. Although exonerated by a court of inquiry in these matters (he was acquitted of "any fault, misconduct or negligence"), it was a serious blow to the confidence of a gifted, yet aging, leader.

The events redirected his field leadership. In the winter of 1778–79, Putnam commanded the troops quartered near Redding before looking after a wing in the west side of the Hudson. His active service would conclude with a fit of paralysis in December 1779; one-half of him was so paralyzed that his right arm clung close and useless to his side, and he had to be assisted to mount his horse. As an American folk hero, Israel Putnam would spend his final years on the family farm, where he passed on May 29, 1790.

Of Putnam Qualities

Author Oliver W.B. Peabody stated that Israel Putnam's leadership "reminds the reader of Murat, the gallant Marshall of Napoleon" and then helps readers remember that Putnam was "wholly without military education and with scarcely any other, and simply by the force of his own energy and talent, he rose through all the gradations of the service to the station of first major-general in the army, till he stood second in rank to Washington alone."[130]

Tenacious? Certainly. Audacious? Clearly. But he was also a savvy yeoman, builder, trader and even craftsman—case in point: Putnam Farm.

A Pomfret Family

On January 7, 1718, Israel Putnam was born to a wealthy family in Salem Village (now Danvers), Massachusetts. His parents, Joseph Putnam (1669–1724) and Elizabeth Porter (1673–1746), cultivated the land with the assistance of a large family: Mary, Sarah, Rachel, William, David, Eunice,

The birthplace of Israel Putnam, Danvers, Massachusetts. *Library of Congress.*

Huldah, Mehitable, Sarah Brown, Elizabeth, Ann and Israel. While the Putnams prospered, they also witnessed the scandalous execution of twenty of their neighbors for witchcraft in the infamous trials of 1692.[131]

The children's grandparents were Thomas Putnam (1614–1686) and Mary Ingersoll (1626–1693) and Israel Porter (1643–1706) and Elizabeth Hawthorne (1649–1706).[132] The children's great-grandparents on their father's side were John Putnam Sr. (circa 1579–1662) and Priscilla Gould (circa 1585–1662) and Lawrence Ingersoll (1605–1645) and Lydia Bentley (1606–1662). On their mother's side, they were John Porter (1596–1676) and Mary Endicott (circa 1598–1684) and William Hawthorne III (1607–1681) and Ann Johnson (1607–1681).

Born into such a large family, Israel learned early the value of persistence and self-reliance. Given only a spattering of education, the young man's interests shifted to the open air of New England, including hunting, farming and self-defense.

Women, too, became a distraction, as Putnam married Hannah Pope in Salem, Massachusetts, on July 19, 1739. Hannah, born on September 3, 1721, was a New Englander at heart and welcomed the opportunity to share her life with Israel on their Putnam Farm. The family grew fruit trees and raised livestock on their 514 acres in Mortlake Manor, in the northeastern corner of Connecticut. From gathering ripened apples to shearing the sheep, Hannah was as happy making a fresh desert as she was stitching a woolen sweater. In the spring of 1743, when an old she-wolf and her puppies destroyed seventy of their valuable sheep and goats, Israel himself would gain notoriety by facing down the wolf in her den and then shooting her with his musket.

A large family of ten children would assist with the family responsibilities.[133] The Putnam daughters were: Hannah (II) (1744–1821), who married John Winchester Dana; Elizabeth (1747–1765);[134] Mehitable (1749–1789), who married Captain Daniel Tyler III (1750–1832);[135] Mary "Molly" (1753–1825), who married Samuel Waldo; and finally Eunice (1756–1799). Israel (1740–1812), the Putnams' firstborn son, married Sarah Waldo. After the battle of Lexington, Israel Putnam Jr. raised a company of volunteers and served under his father. Appointed as his father's aide on July 22, 1775, he filled that position for three years. He, along with his third cousin, Rufus Putnam, were among the veterans seeking western lands as payment for their military service, known as the Ohio Company of Associates. Other Putnam sons were Daniel "David" (1742–1758);[136] Daniel (II) (1759–1831); David (1761–1761), who died at the age of one month and seven days;[137] and Peter Schuyler Putnam (1764–1827), who married Lucy Frink. Peter, named after one of Israel's compatriots in the French and Indian War, would eventually run an inn with his family and settle in Williamstown, Massachusetts.

Israel's spouse, Hannah, would pass on April 6, 1765, at the age of forty-three.[138]

DEBORAH AVERY PUTNAM

On June 3, 1767, Colonel Putnam married Deborah Lathrop Avery Gardiner. It was the third marriage for the wealthy widow of John Gardiner and the second for Putnam. The two had known each other for years and often shared tales of their experiences among a similar circle of friends. As Colonel Putnam was one of the most popular men of his days, their home, as one might imagine, drew throngs of visitors. So much so that it encouraged the couple to move from their rural home to the Avery estate in Brooklyn, their hope being to convert the spacious property into an inn. Presided over by the dignified Mrs. Putnam, the successful establishment soon became the most noted gathering place in eastern Connecticut.[139]

The daughter of Samuel and Deborah (Crow) Lathrop (or Lothrop), Deborah was born on January 9, 1719, in Norwich.[140] Reverend John Lothrop, the first representative of the family in New England, was her great-great-grandfather. At nineteen years of age, Deborah married Reverend Ephraim Avery (1713–1754), the son of Reverend John Avery and Ruth Little. The couple settled comfortably into the Second Church at Pomfret (now called Brooklyn) and had nine children—three daughters and six sons, one of whom died in infancy.

When a malignant form of dysentery swept the area in 1754, it claimed not only the life of Deborah's five-year-old boy, Septimus, but also that of her husband. Nevertheless, the widow with seven children persisted with the assistance of friends and family until she met John Gardiner (1714–1764), also called Lord Gardiner, the fifth proprietor of Gardiner's Island. The couple had two children before Mr. Gardiner passed in 1764.

While at Israel Putnam's headquarters on the Hudson in 1777, Deborah Avery Putnam died.

THE CORE FOUR

Along with Charles Lee, Philip Schuyler and Artemas Ward, Israel Putnam was one of the four major generals in the Continental army chosen to assist in the conversion of militia units into a military force. Appointed by the Continental Congress on June 19, 1775, it was a near impossible task for the quartet, considering the conditions—the lack of discipline, food, hygiene, salaries, supplies, training and uniforms.

The controversial Charles Lee, often of questioned allegiance, was born in England. Living in Virginia for only two years before the war, his military credentials carried him to his appointment but could sustain him no further. By the end of 1776, the man whom Fort Lee is named after began criticizing George Washington—the very man who had given him that honor. Captured by the British, traded and disgraced at Monmouth, Lee's court-martial stripped him of his military respect.

A delegate to the Continental Congress before his selection, Philip Schuyler was placed in command of the Northern Department in New

Along with Lee, Schuyler and Ward, Israel Putnam (pictured here) was one of the four major generals in the Continental army chosen to establish a military force.

York. There, he prepared to invade Canada. But his health failed, and the actual command devolved to General Richard Montgomery. From this point forward, Schuyler's military career waned. Although acquitted of every charge during a 1778 court-martial, he resigned from the army in 1779 to pursue his political aspirations.

Never in good stead with George Washington, nor in good health, Artemas Ward was forced to resign from the army on March 20, 1777. He then turned to public office, which included his selection as a delegate to the Continental Congress and, later, a role as Massachusetts Speaker of the House during Shays' Rebellion in 1786.

For Israel Putnam, this appointment, along with his distinguished service at the Battle of Bunker Hill—which included his strategic fortifications for Breed's Hill—confirmed his value and placed him into proper historical context.[141] As for the associated idiom, "Do not fire until you see the whites of their eyes," well, it was a common turn of phrase used by eighteenth-century officers to control fire.[142] This said, it does not diminish (to some, the locution is an embellishment of the Revolutionary hero) in any manner Putnam's enormous contribution. For years, people would travel to Israel Putnam's aboveground tomb, in Brooklyn's South Cemetery, to remove a chip from the impressive marble slab that marked the grave.[143] That's how powerful an image this man had created and why, to this very day, people are drawn to nearby historical societies in hopes of discovering lineage to the Putnam family.

Chapter 12

THE REEVE FAMILY OF LITCHFIELD

The Litchfield Law School was one of the first fruits of the American Revolution.
—Simeon E. Baldwin, former Connecticut governor, August 1, 1920

The evidence will show that this man, Tapping Reeve, was not only an adept attorney but also a master in the field of legal education. From his convincing argument in the case of *Brom and Bett v. Ashley* to his prescient Litchfield Law School, his civic pride was unmatched and his patriotism incontrovertible.

Born in Brookhaven, New York, in October 1744, Tapping Reeve graduated from the College of New Jersey (Princeton University) in 1763. While earning his master's (completed in 1766), he taught locally before heading across Long Island Sound and into the colony of Connecticut. There, he would study law under the esteemed Judge Jesse Root, also a College of New Jersey graduate. Admitted to the bar in 1772, Reeve began practicing law in the growing (the population of the town had grown to 2,544 in 1774, from 1,366 in 1756) commercial center of Litchfield, west of Hartford.

As Reeve's legal reputation grew, so, too, did his patriotism, or so it seemed. He took an active interest in serving his community and was appointed by the Connecticut Assembly to rouse support, or "drum up volunteers," for the Revolution. The young attorney even accepted an officer's commission in the Continental army but never saw battle. In 1788, Reeve was nominated the state's attorney—this on the strength of his service in the legislature and on the governor's council.

The earliest American law school was conducted under the watchful eyes of both Tapping Reeve and James Gould. *Library of Congress.*

As a fervent Federalist, Reeve would not be silent, nor would he stand in the shadow of his opposition. It simply wasn't his nature. During the 1790s, he set quill to paper in many an article in favor of both the Washington and Adams administrations; his impassioned position even landed him an 1806 grand jury indictment for libeling President Thomas Jefferson. Thankfully, not only for Reeve but also his opponents, it was dismissed.

BROM AND BETT V. ASHLEY

In 1781, Reeve had the opportunity to work with Theodore Sedgwick to defend a Sheffield, Massachusetts slave named Elizabeth Freeman (known as Mum Bett). Born a slave, Bett had listened to discussions related to the

Massachusetts Constitution and had heard the phrase "all men are born free and equal." She then claimed her freedom from her former master. Two years later, Sedgwick and Reeve would successfully employ this argument in court to secure her freedom. This case, (*Brom and Bett v. Ashley*) would set a precedent that would later lead to the abolition of slavery in Massachusetts.

THE LITCHFIELD LAW SCHOOL

Far more than an attorney, Tapping Reeve was a legal seer. As was customary, he also offered apprenticeships, but he, like his mentor, Root, wanted to impart more. The value of such a relationship, he felt, could be ameliorated—a more structured approach would improve the experience. In 1784, in what would

Illustrious alumni from inside these walls included 28 U.S. senators, 101 members of the House of Representatives, 14 governors and 16 state chief justices.

Litchfield Law School graduate Ward Hunt, associate justice of the U.S. Supreme Court from 1872 to 1882. *Library of Congress.*

prove to be his legal legacy, he built a small schoolhouse next to his home. This schoolhouse became the Litchfield Law School, the first such institution in the United States. For an annual cost of $350—$100 for tuition and $250 for board and expenses—a student could receive an extraordinary legal education. Graduation, often a fourteen-month process, combined an aggressive reading and writing regimen within a simulated legal milieu.

Top: Litchfield Law School scholar Levi Woodbury, associate justice of the U.S. Supreme Court from 1845 to 1851. *Library of Congress*.

Right: Litchfield Law School graduate Horace Mann, member of the U.S. House of Representatives from 1848 to 1853. *Library of Congress*.

From 1784 to 1833, interest in the school grew with each prestigious graduate.[144] Two academics, Aaron Burr and John Calhoun, would go on to serve their country in the role of vice president.[145] But there would be more: three would serve on the U.S. Supreme Court (Henry Baldwin, Levi Woodbury and Ward Hunt), and six would become cabinet members. Other illustrious alumni included 28 U.S. senators, 101 members of the House of Representatives, 14 governors and 16 state chief justices. Impressive as this may sound, the most extraordinary achievement belonged to its master, Tapping Reeve, who during the first fourteen years taught alone.[146]

CIVIC PRIDE

While teaching, Reeve was named a judge of the Connecticut Superior Court (1798), and in 1814, he became chief justice of the Court of Errors.[147] He retired in 1816 to devote all of his time to writing, family law being of paramount interest to the scholar.[148]

LYMAN BEECHER

Reeve also became known for bringing Reverend Lyman Beecher (a great preacher and the father of an even greater one), a noted adversary of Unitarianism, to serve as pastor of the Litchfield Congregational Church in 1810. Dr. Beecher, who developed a strong bond with the legal authority, even held special theology classes for Reeve's students.[149]

Lyman's son, Henry Ward Beecher, would become the most celebrated Calvinist minister of his day. He would leave the rolling hills of Litchfield County for the flatlands of Indiana. Of his brothers and sisters, all of whom shared a passion for education and activism, Harriet Beecher Stowe would garner the greatest attention.

FAMILY COURT

While earning his master's degree, Tapping Reeve tutored the two orphaned children of Reverend Aaron Burr and his wife, Esther Edwards Burr: Aaron Burr Jr., the future vice president of the United States, and Sarah, known also as Sally. The two children had been left in the care of an uncle. Enthralled with young Sarah, Tapping Reeve married the seventeen-year-old on June 4, 1771.

Aaron Burr Reeve, the only child of Tapping and Sarah, was born on October 3, 1780. Graduating from Yale in 1802, he would become an attorney in Troy, New York. Marrying Annabella Sheldon, of New York, on November 21, 1801, the couple would make their home near his practice. The Reeves had one son, Tapping Burr Reeve, who died at the young age of twenty on August 28, 1829 (he had been studying at Yale and died in Litchfield). Aaron Burr Reeve died in 1809, and Annabella Reeve later married David Burr of New Haven.

An invalid, Sarah Reeve struggled with her health for years and died on March 30, 1797. Tapping then married Elizabeth Thompson in 1799, but

The Tapping Reeve House, in Litchfield, is adjacent to the Litchfield Law School, and together they have been designated a National Historic Landmark.

the couple had no children. On December 13, 1823, Tapping Reeve died in Litchfield and was buried alongside Sally. Elizabeth passed on December 13, 1842, and was buried alongside Tapping.

AARON BURR (1756–1836)

Born on February 6, 1756, Aaron Burr would be raised by his uncle Timothy Edwards, who lived in Elizabethtown, New Jersey.[150] It would be Edwards who would see to Burr's proper education. So gifted a youth, Burr would be ready for college at age eleven. But Princeton refused his early admission, and he had to wait until 1769, two years later. When the teenager graduated in 1772, he pondered many directions, including the Presbyterian world chosen by both his father and grandfather. But as fate would have it, he ended up back with Tapping Reeve, this time at the Litchfield Law School.

Ignited by the Lexington alarm, Burr joined the Continental army during the summer of 1775. He took part in Benedict Arnold's expedition to Canada; assisted General Richard Montgomery, who promoted him to captain; and distinguished himself at the Battle of Quebec.

Burr then found himself, albeit briefly (six weeks), as an aide to General Washington before serving bravely under Connecticut's own General Israel Putnam in New York. Later, at the sun-scorched Battle of Monmouth, Burr was a brigade commander in Lord Sterling's division. On March 10, 1779, he resigned from the Continental army and resumed his law studies. Fond of his military exploits, Burr never balked at an opportunity to share them, using them to his advantage in a court of law.[151]

By 1782, he had passed the bar and married Theodosia Bartow Prevost (1746–1794), a graceful widow with five children. She was ten years older and the former spouse of British army officer Jacques Marcus Prevost. The couple lived in Albany before moving to New York City, where Burr would build his reputation as a trial attorney before turning to public service. Later, during Burr's unsuccessful presidential bid of 1800, a prominent state official would state, "Had Aaron Burr not aroused prejudice by marrying a British wife, he would have been elected President by a large majority."[152]

There was much mutual respect between the Burrs. It was said that "his married life with Mrs. Prevost was of the most affectionate character, and his

Two graduates, Aaron Burr (pictured here) and John Calhoun, would go on to serve their country in the role of vice president. *Library of Congress.*

fidelity never questioned…He was always a gentleman in his language and deportment…[he] had a special regard for the maxim that 'things written remain,' and was careful as to what he wrote."[153]

When Burr's spouse passed, it left him with their only child together, Theodosia, named after her mother. The young girl was an outstanding student—the perfect complement to Burr's belief in education equality for women. In 1801, she married Governor Joseph Alston of South Carolina, and the couple had a son who died at the young age of ten. Tragically, Theodosia disappeared aboard the schooner *Patriot* off the Carolina coast during the winter of 1812–13.[154]

When Aaron Burr defeated General Philip Schuyler, Alexander Hamilton's father-in-law, for a seat in the U.S. Senate in 1791, it was the turning point in what would become a bitter rivalry between Burr and Hamilton. Six years later, Burr, battling against the same opponent, lost his reelection bid—the defeat blamed not on the voters or his opponent but on Hamilton for his disparaging remarks. While the loss might have discouraged most, it ignited Burr. In 1800, he ran unsuccessfully against Thomas Jefferson for the U.S. presidency and became vice president instead. Since both had had the same amount of electoral votes, members of the House of Representatives were left to determine the winner. Again, Hamilton turned up and voiced his disapproval of Burr; the election went to Jefferson and Burr's detestation to Hamilton.

As Burr's vice presidential days ended, he turned his attention to the governorship of New York but lost the election to Morgan Lewis. Once more, Hamilton was to blame.

Aaron Burr challenged Alexander Hamilton to a duel on the morning of July 7, 1804. Their rivalry ended when Burr's antagonist received a mortal wound from which he died after thirty-one hours of intense suffering. While the vice president felt he had defended his honor, the public felt differently. Their "murderous" cries, however, did not prohibit Burr from finishing his term.

Three years later, in an unrelated incident, as they say, Burr was brought to trial on charges of conspiracy and high misdemeanor but was acquitted of wrongdoing. The scandal—which involved garnering support for revolutionizing Mexico and freeing the Spanish colonies—put an end to his political career.[155]

Later, he practiced law in New York and married a wealthy young widow, Eliza Jumel, in 1833. The marriage—annulled after only a few months—failed, as did Burr's health, and he died under the care of his cousin on September 14, 1836, on Staten Island.

JONATHAN EDWARDS

Esther Edwards Burr, Aaron Burr's mother and Tapping Reeve's mother-in-law, was the daughter of the most gifted theologian of the Great Awakening, Jonathan Edwards.[156]

Born to pastor Timothy and Esther Edwards on October 5, 1703, in East Windsor, Jonathan Edwards was the only son in a family of eleven children. He entered Yale in 1716—before he was a teenager—and graduated four years later. Three years after that, Edwards received his master's.

Unable to accept the Calvinist sovereignty of God, Edwards found his guidance, acknowledged it and turned to Christ. Ordained a minister at Northampton, in 1727, he assisted Solomon Stoddard, his maternal grandfather, while continuing his studies. It was during that period that he married Sarah Pierrepont (also spelled Pierpont), the seventeen-year-old daughter of James Pierrepont (1659–1714), a founder of the Collegiate School (Yale University). The couple, too, would have a large family of eleven children.

When Stoddard died, on February 11, 1729, his grandson became the sole minister of the church. It was an incredible challenge for young Edwards but one that would transform the largest and wealthiest congregations in the colony into religious epicenters. The First Great Awakening, of the 1730s and 1740s, saw Edwards at the heart of change. But it was not without controversy, as his disagreement with some of his grandfather's practices, such as open communion, caused his dismissal in 1750.

Edwards then headed to the frontier settlement of Stockbridge, Massachusetts, where he found consolation for his work. A smaller congregation allowed him more time not only for his writing but also for his missionary work, including that of the Housatonic Indians. Jonathan Edwards's most celebrated work, *The Freedom of Will*, would be penned at the outpost in 1754.

Early in 1758, the most eminent American philosopher of his time became president of the College of New Jersey (later Princeton University). Before Edwards could affect the institution, however, he came down with a fever and died on March 22, 1758. His final resting place is in the President's Lot in the Princeton cemetery beside his son-in-law, Aaron Burr.

Summation

It has not been uncommon for historians to compare Connecticut's Tapping Reeve with Virginia's own George Wythe, pronounced (w̌ith), the noted classics scholar and distinguished judge; the parallels—including everything from each being married twice and having only one son to their relentless commitment to their craft—are indeed striking. Of the two brilliant legal minds, however, Wythe, who penned his name on the Declaration of Independence, is the better known.[157]

But in fairness, both tend to be forgotten, unless, of course, you find yourself walking the streets of Litchfield or Williamsburg.

Like Wythe, Reeve's family became his students. Certainly this was the case with Burr, but it was no less true for the many other minds he influenced, whose intellect would go on to forge the foundation of liberty and to ensure the natural and equal rights of man. To their credit, both scholars discerned that professional study needed competent teaching and then let their souls shepherd them toward that goal.

Let it be said, on behalf of every Revolutionary family of Connecticut, that few deserve a greater debt of gratitude for their endowment to the cornerstone of our nation than Tapping Reeve.

Chapter 13

THE SHERMAN FAMILY
OF NEW HAVEN

The question is, not what rights naturally belong to man, but how they may be most equally and effectually guarded in society.
—Roger Sherman

When Roger Sherman (a man the great orator Patrick Henry regarded as one of the three greatest men at the Constitutional Convention) signed his name to all four of the great state papers—the (Continental) Association of 1774, the Declaration of Independence, the Articles of Confederation and the U.S. Constitution—he separated himself from his peers and became "The Countryman."[158]

Born near the Skinner place, on Waverly Avenue, as it was often recalled, in Newton, Massachusetts, on April 19, 1721, Sherman became a self-made man. Learning quickly that his "common" school attendance and shoemaker's apprenticeship would not separate himself from the other children of Stoughton (his family hometown located seventeen miles from Boston), he turned toward education.[159] And he did so at his own pace, using his father's library and the advice of his parish minister.[160] For Sherman, scholarship became a passion, even allowing him to become a self-taught mathematician.

When his father passed (1743), the family moved to New Milford, Connecticut, where his older brother had become a merchant. In partnership with his sibling, he opened the town's first store and also became active in civic affairs (all three branches of Connecticut government—legislative, executive and judicial—would benefit from his

A wood engraving, from sketches by I.E. Hurlburt, depicting Mayor Roger Sherman of New Haven. *Library of Congress.*

influence before the war even began).[161]As treasurer of Yale University, he was a paragon of efficiency, and it gained him an honorary master of arts degree (1768). Later, he was elected the first mayor of New Haven, a post he held until his death.[162]

FAMILY MATTERS

Roger Sherman married Elizabeth Hartwell (1726–1760), the eldest daughter of Deacon Joseph Hartwell of Stoughton, on November 17, 1749. The couple produced seven children. John (born 1750) served in the war as a lieutenant and paymaster and died at Canton, Massachusetts, on August

8, 1802. He was father to Reverend John Sherman of Trenton Falls. William (born 1751), a 1770 Yale graduate, served also as a lieutenant and paymaster. He married and had one daughter. Isaac (born 1753), who graduated with his brother from Yale, served as a lieutenant colonel and commandant. Fighting bravely at New Rochelle, Trenton, Princeton, Monmouth and Stony Point, he died unmarried in 1819. Chloe (first of this name, 1754–1757) and Oliver (1756–1757) died young. Chloe (second of this name, born 1758) married Dr. John Skinner, a New Haven physician, and had one son, Roger Sherman Skinner. Last born was Elizabeth (1760–1762), who also died young.[163]

On October 19, 1760, Elizabeth died at just thirty-four years of age. She was respected, of good character and firm in her Christian belief. Devastated by the loss, Roger closed his law practice, resigned his judgeship and moved to New Haven.

Later, Sherman married Rebecca Minot Prescott (1742–1813), daughter of Benjamin Prescott of Danvers, Massachusetts, on May 12, 1763.[164] She was half his age. Eight children—five daughters and three sons—were the fruit of this marriage. Rebecca (born 1764) married Judge Simeon Baldwin of New Haven, a member of Congress from Connecticut and judge of the Supreme Court. Elizabeth (born 1765), married first Sturges Burr and then, following the death of her sister Rebecca, Judge Simeon Baldwin. The couple produced one son, Simeon, a New York merchant. Roger (born 1768) was a 1787 Yale graduate and a New Haven broker. Mehetabel (first of this name, 1772) died young, while a second Mehetabel (born 1774) married wholesaler Daniel Barnes, the couple producing one son. She then married Jeremiah Evarts and had one child, the Honorable William M. Evarts. Oliver (born 1777) graduated from Yale in 1795, became a Boston agent and is said to have died of yellow fever in the West Indies in 1820. Martha (born 1779) married Jeremiah Day, DD, president of Yale College. Lastly, Sarah (born 1783) married Samuel Hoar of Concord, Massachusetts.[165]

Resolute, unswerving and self-sacrificing, Rebecca Prescott Sherman assumed full responsibility for all the children, including those of her husband's former marriage. Described as a beautiful woman of charm, good humor and common sense, her internal qualities ran deeper—not surprising, considering her lineage; she was a descendant of John Prescott, one of the first settlers of Worcester County, Massachusetts, and Colonel William Prescott of Bunker Hill fame.

Once welcomed to a dinner party hosted by General Washington, Rebecca was given the seat of honor, to the general's right. It was from there that she drew the disdain of Madam Hancock. Hearing of the slight, Washington replied that "it was his privilege to give his arm to the handsomest woman in the room."[166]

It has been said that Rebecca even assisted in sewing some of the stars on the very first flag of this nation and was selected, along with Mrs. Wooster, to make the first flag ever in the state of Connecticut.[167] As a trusted advisor, Roger never hesitated to consult her on both public and private matters—a fact that speaks volumes. Sherman often quipped, "He never liked to decide a perplexing question without submitting it for the opinion of some intelligent woman."[168]

Of the Signers, Robert Treat Paine and Roger Sherman were fifth cousins once removed (through the Shermans). Of the spouses of the Signers, Mrs. Dorothy Quincy Hancock Scott, wife firstly of John Hancock, was a half-second cousin once removed of Mrs. Abigail Smith Adams (through the Quincys) and a fourth cousin, through the Hoars, of both Mrs. Adams and Mrs. Rebecca Prescott Sherman, second wife of Roger Sherman.[169]

SIMEON BALDWIN (1761–1851)

Born in Norwich, Connecticut, on December 14, 1761, Simeon graduated from Yale College in 1781. He then tutored, studied law and was admitted to the bar in 1786. Practicing in New Haven led to his appointment as clerk of the district and circuit courts of the United States for the district of Connecticut (1790–1803). It was a position he held until he was elected to the Eighth Congress. Simeon Baldwin, a son-in-law of Roger Sherman, would return to the courts before his election as mayor of New Haven in 1826.

ROGER SHERMAN BALDWIN (1793–1863)

Roger Sherman Baldwin—son of Simeon Baldwin, grandson of Roger Sherman and cousin of William Maxwell Evarts, George Frisbie Hoar and Ebenezer Rockwood Hoar—was born in New Haven on January 4, 1793. A Yale graduate of 1811, Baldwin studied at the Litchfield Law School and was admitted to the New Haven Bar in 1814. Independently minded, opting for his own legal firm over that of a traditional partnership, he quickly honed his legal skills.

Like his father, Baldwin was an ardent opponent of slavery and didn't balk at the opportunity to prove it. From defending a runaway slave to gaining national recognition for his defense of the African prisoners in the *Amistad* case, Baldwin was relentless in his support of human rights. In the latter case—one that became an international incident—Baldwin served alongside John Quincy Adams, the former president of the United States. Before the U.S. Supreme Court, Baldwin delivered a powerful oratory (one of the most impressive arguments of his day) on the basic liberties of human beings and the free status, especially in the United States, of the illegally enslaved. When it was followed by the moving summation of John Quincy Adams, it persuaded the justices of the Supreme Court, in the spring of 1841, to make the illegally transported (Mende African) captives free people once more.

Prior to becoming the governor of Connecticut (1844–46), Baldwin served on the New Haven Common Council (1826), the New Haven Board of Alderman (1827) and the Connecticut General Assembly (1837–38, 1840–41). As governor, while he fought for education, election and immigration reform, it was his battle against slavery that really marked his term. In 1844, Baldwin sought a law to end slavery in Connecticut and one that would permit free blacks to vote. But both failed during his term.[170] Two years after he left office, and while he was serving in the United States Senate (1847–51), slavery was finally abolished in Connecticut (1848).

He passed on February 19, 1863, in New Haven.

WILLIAM M. EVARTS (1818–1901), GRANDSON OF ROGER SHERMAN

Appointed secretary of state by President Rutherford B. Hayes on March 7, 1877, William M. Evarts, the grandson of Roger Sherman, served until March 7, 1881. Born in Boston on February 6, 1818, he was an 1837 Yale College graduate. Upon returning to Boston, he turned toward Harvard Law School (1838). Two years later, Evarts moved to New York City, where he was admitted to the bar on July 16, 1841.

His foray into politics came with an appointment as assistant district attorney of the southern district of New York (1848–53). Feeling a calling to public service, Evarts was uncertain just how to attain it; he soon abandoned his Whig party principles for that of the newly formed Republican Party. An unsuccessful 1861 Senate bid turned him away from politics and back toward the legal field. There, Evarts embellished his reputation as one of the country's top lawyers.

National prominence came to the attorney when he was retained as counsel to President Andrew Johnson during his impeachment trial. The U.S. House of Representatives impeached the president on February 24, 1868. The trial concluded on May 16, 1868, with Johnson's acquittal, with the votes for conviction being one less than the required two-thirds tally. Afterward, Johnson appointed Evarts as attorney general (July 16, 1868–March 4, 1869).

Evarts returned to his private practice, always a safe haven, before representing (in the disputed 1876 election) the Republican Party before the Hayes-Tilden commission. This role, too, led to better opportunities, as Evarts was nominated for secretary of state. His public service role ended as a United States senator from New York (1885–91). William M. Evarts died on February 28, 1901.

SARAH AND SAMUEL HOAR

When Sarah Sherman married Samuel Hoar (1778–1856), it introduced another branch into the powerful Sherman family. Born in Lincoln, Massachusetts, Samuel Hoar was an 1802 Harvard College graduate and was as enterprising as he was determined. Admitted to the bar in 1805, he married eight years later and then began his political career as a delegate to the 1820 Massachusetts Constitutional Convention. A powerful Whig member of the state senate (1826, 1832–33), Hoar then used his position as a springboard into the United States House of Representatives for the Fourth Massachusetts District (1835–37). Known for his maritime expertise and antislavery views, Hoar returned to the state house of representatives in 1850. He passed six years later.

The Hoars had five surviving children (of six offspring): Elizabeth (1814–1878) was engaged to Charles Chauncey Emerson (1808–1836), the younger brother of Ralph Waldo Emerson, who died before they could marry; Ebenezer (1816–1895), a Harvard graduate (1835) and associate justice of the

The Fiftieth Congress Massachusetts Delegation featured George Frisbie Hoar.
Library of Congress.

Massachusetts Supreme Court, married Caroline Brooks; Sarah (1817–1907) married Boston importer Robert Boyd Storer; Samuel Johnson (1820–1821) died in infancy; Edward Sherman (1823–1892), also a Harvard graduate (1844), married Elizabeth Hallet Prichard and was a friend and neighbor of Henry David Thoreau; and George Frisbie Hoar (1826–1904) was a Harvard graduate (1845) and prominent United States senator from Massachusetts.

ROGER SHERMAN'S FINEST HOURS

On September 5, 1774, the first session of the Continental Congress convened—with delegates from twelve colonies (all except Georgia)—at Carpenter's Hall in Philadelphia. For Connecticut's part, it had elected Eliphalet Dyer, William S. Johnson, Erastus Wolcott, Silas Deane and Richard Law. When Johnson, Wolcott and Law declined, Roger Sherman and Joseph Trumbull were elected. Only Dyer, Sherman and Deane attended the congress.

When this congress was dissolved, a second followed on May 10, 1775. Again, Dyer, Sherman and Deane represented Connecticut, but now the times had changed. On April 19, 1775, the British regulars had happened upon a group of American soldiers at Lexington, and shots had been fired. Royal troops had been shut up in Boston, and Ticonderoga and Crown Point were under new ownership. Sherman was not silent. Although the selection of George Washington as commander-in-chief was unanimous, he had hoped to secure Major General David Wooster to command the Connecticut forces.[171] Instead, General Israel Putnam was the selection.

As a prolific committee member, Sherman saw to military operations in Canada, trade and currency regulation, military supply logistics, providing for government expenses and the preparation of articles of confederation between several states. He, along with Adams, Franklin, Jefferson and Livingston, was also on the drafting committee for the Declaration of Independence.

As the second-oldest delegate, following only eighty-one-year-old Franklin, Sherman joined fellow Connecticut delegates Dr. William Samuel Johnson and Oliver Ellsworth at the Constitutional Convention of 1787. Advocating its adoption, Sherman—responsible for the Great Compromise (Connecticut Compromise)—believed it a proper extension of civil liberty and political prosperity.[172]

On July 23, 1793, while still serving as senator from Connecticut, Roger Sherman died of typhoid at the age of seventy-two.

THE SHERMAN AURA

Sherman's sheer presence commanded respect, perhaps no more so than as a part of a judicial or legislative body. A man of deliberate remarks, he delivered

A marker, "In Memory of the Honorable Roger Sherman," at the family burial plot at Grove Street Cemetery in New Haven.

them slowly and in a methodical manner. Far from a gifted orator, his succinct comments spoke volumes—so much so that even if his colleagues, such as Fisher Ames, missed the discussion of a topic and thus did not know in which direction to vote, they would side with their conscience, Roger Sherman.[173]

Of his contemporary, John Adams wrote:

The honorable Roger Sherman was one of the most cordial friends which I ever had in my life...he was one of the most sensible men in the world. The clearest head and steadiest heart. It is praise enough to say, that the late Chief Justice Ellsworth told me he had made Mr. Sherman his model in his youth. Indeed I never knew two men more alike, except that the Chief Justice had the advantage of a liberal education and somewhat more extensive reading.[174]

A pious man of integrity, Sherman did not drift from his principles. A devout Christian, he became a respected theologian and stood among some of the most distinguished divines of the period. His self-control and evenness of temper enabled him to stay on good terms even with those whose views differed radically from his.

Chapter 14

THE TALLMADGE FAMILY
OF LITCHFIELD

This year [1778] *I opened a private correspondence with some persons in New York*
[for General Washington] *which lasted through the war. How beneficial it was
to the Commander-in-Chief is evidenced by his continuing the same to the close of the
war. I kept one or more boats continually employed crossing the Sound on business.*
*—memoir of Colonel Benjamin Tallmadge, and an abstruse reference to the
Culper Spy Ring*[175]

The Reverend Benjamin Tallmadge (1725–1786) married the eminent
Susannah Smith (1729–68) on May 16, 1750. Susannah was the
daughter of Reverend John Smith, of White Plains, New York, and Mehitable
Hooker. She was also the great-granddaughter of William Leete, governor
of both the New Haven Colony (1661–65) and of the Connecticut Colony
(1670–76), and a great-granddaughter of the Reverend Thomas Hooker,
"Founder of the state of Connecticut and father of its Constitution." And
there was more: Susannah was the great-granddaughter of Captain Thomas
Willett, the first mayor of New York. Her grandfather Thomas Smith was
one of the founders of the First Presbyterian Church in New York, and
her uncle William Smith was justice of the Supreme Court of New York
Province and one of the incorporators of Princeton College and the New
York Society Library.

Reverend Tallmadge was born on January 1, 1725. Graduating from
Yale College in 1747, he taught at the Hopkins Grammar School while

Benjamin Tallmadge passed on March 7, 1835, and was interred in Litchfield's East Cemetery.

fulfilling his theological studies for ordainment. Filling the vacant pulpit at Brookhaven, or Setauket, Long Island, the family quickly found themselves a home. There, they would raise a family of five boys: William (1752–1776), Benjamin (II) (1754–1835), Samuel (1755–1825), John (1757–1823) and Isaac (1762–unknown).

On January 3, 1770, nearly two years after the death of Susannah, Reverend Tallmadge married Zipporah Strong, daughter of Thomas Strong, of Brookhaven, and Susanna Thompson. They had no children. Upon his death, Zipporah Strong Tallmadge married again and survived until June 13, 1835.

THREE BROTHERS IN ARMS

Benjamin's three elder sons all served in the American Revolution. William, the eldest son, served in Captain Hubbell's Company of Colonel Huntington's Connecticut Continental Regiment. At the Battle of Long Island, he was one of many from that unit taken prisoner. He would die in the sordid conditions of a British prison. Benjamin (II) is detailed in the paragraphs that follow. The third son was Samuel, who from 1776 to the end of 1780 was attached to the Fourth New York Regiment and eventually made a sergeant in Captain Sackett's Company. In 1777, he participated in the Battle of Saratoga and witnessed Burgoyne's surrender. From that point forward, he was aggressively promoted and reached first lieutenant on October 27, 1781. His records state that he was mustered out of the army in June 1783.[176]

A SON EVER SO HUMBLE

Given his father's name at Brookhaven, where he was born on February 25, 1754, Benjamin Tallmadge was handsome, tenacious and shrewd. The value of education and service, be it to God or country, was foremost in the Tallmadge household, an edict not taken lightly by young Benjamin, who entered Yale College in the autumn of 1769 and graduated in 1773.[177] He then assumed the role of superintendent of Wethersfield High School (1773–76), a position left vacant with the retirement of David Humphreys, Esq. "Electrified" by the bloodshed at Lexington and again at Bunker Hill, Tallmadge was offered commission as a lieutenant in the Continental Line on June 20, 1776.[178] While in New York City, his first assignment, Tallmadge would witness the awful scene of battle and the destruction of his fellow citizen. He later wrote, "I will remember my sensations on the occasion, for they were solemn beyond description, and very hardly could I bring my mind to be willing to attempt the life of a fellow-creature."[179]

Although awakened to the consequences of war, Tallmadge would not balk at engagement. Soon he was offered leadership of the first troop in the second regiment of light dragoons (cavalrymen) commanded by Colonel Elisha Sheldon. As the appointment came from General George Washington

Although not the original owner, Benjamin Tallmadge added elegance to his high-style Georgian home with the addition of porticos in 1782.

himself, Tallmadge was "highly honored."[180]Aggressively promoted, he would make colonel by September 5, 1779.

In the summer of 1778, at the height of the Revolution, Benjamin Tallmadge began constructing a sophisticated intelligence lattice that would operate within the British-occupied region of New York City. The Culper Ring (the name was derived from the aliases taken by two of its main members, Abraham Woodhull and Robert Townsend, who were respectively known as "Samuel Culper Sr." and "Samuel Culper Jr.") would serve to validate Tallmadge, who would then report directly to Washington as intelligence czar. The covert operations of the group would remain essentially unknown for years, with even its leader offering little insight.[181]

Tallmadge, too, played a major role in the capture of Major John Andre, adjutant general to the British army, who had been conspiring with turncoat General Benedict Arnold. While Tallmadge's accomplishments were many—he was forever proud of his attack on Fort St. George (Mastic), Long Island, in November 1780—he drew the greatest amount of satisfaction from being on the staff of General George Washington, a man whom he revered. Later, he would state, "I can truly say that the loss of my own father did not so sensibly affect me as has the death of this peerless man."[182]

After the war, Benjamin Tallmadge returned home to Long Island, where he, along with others who had served, delighted in the gratitude they received. Of the many pleasing and delightful visitors he received during the autumn and winter of 1783, one in particular stood out, Mary Floyd. She was the eldest daughter of Signer William Floyd, of Mastic, Long Island. Benjamin and Mary's nuptials were solemnized on March 18, 1784, and officiated by Benjamin's honored father. Though their love was very deep, it was also very private. Mary was strong in spirit, cultured and mannerly. After a visit to New York and returning back to Mastic, the couple departed for Litchfield, Connecticut.

While living in Litchfield, Benjamin Tallmadge was appointed postmaster (1792), entered the banking industry and was elected as a Federalist to seven succeeding congresses (March 4, 1801–March 3, 1817). In her forty-second year, Mary died on June 3, 1805. Together, the couple had seven children. Colonel Tallmadge then married Maria Hallet, daughter of his old friend Joseph Hallet, of New York, on May 3, 1808. His war memories were confined to a role as treasurer and later president of the Society of the Cincinnati. However, a brief memoir, initiated by his children, drew some attention to the humble soldier. He passed on March 7, 1835, and was interred in Litchfield's East Cemetery. Maria Hallet Tallmadge lived until September 18, 1838.

THE CHILDREN OF BENJAMIN AND MARY TALLMADGE

The eldest son, Colonel William Smith Tallmadge (1785–1822), was born in Litchfield and served as lieutenant colonel of the Forty-sixth United States Infantry during the War of 1812. He died unmarried in Moscow, New York, in 1822.

Henry Floyd Tallmadge (1787–1854), also born in Litchfield, became a businessman and politician. He took the hand of Maria Canfield Adams, daughter of Andrew Adams Jr. of Litchfield. The couple had five children who survived to adulthood.[183]

A painting of Mary Floyd Tallmadge (with children). *Litchfield Historical Society, Litchfield, Connecticut [#1917-04-2]*.

A portrait miniature of Elizabeth
Canfield Tallmadge (1792–1878).
*Litchfield Historical Society, Litchfield,
Connecticut [CA1910-01-1].*

Maria Jones Tallmadge (1790–1878) married John Paine Cushman, of
Troy, a judge of the State Circuit Court in 1812.[184] He died on September
16, 1848, and Maria passed on March 19, 1878, in Troy, New York. The
couple is believed to have had eight children.

Benjamin H. Tallmadge (III) (1792–1831) served in the military and was
an honorary member of the Yale class of 1830. He died unmarried near
Gibraltar on June 20, 1831, while serving in the United States Navy.

Frederick Augustus Tallmadge (1794–1869) was born in Litchfield and
graduated from Yale in 1811. In the War of 1812, he served as a private
in Captain Craig's company of Independent Hussars, New York militia,
for which he received a land warrant. Later, he became a successful lawyer
and a member of Congress and was well known as judge or recorder of
New York City. Frederick married Elizabeth Canfield, the daughter of
Judson Canfield, of Sharon, Connecticut, on May 22, 1815. One of the

most striking couples in Litchfield—the "Rose of Sharon," as Elizabeth was called, was as alluring as she was beautiful, and Frederick had the handsome features of his father—they turned many heads in the small town. The couple had five children: Eliza, Julia, William, Frederick and Mary. Frederick Tallmadge died in Litchfield in 1869. Eliza passed on December 1, 1878, in New York City.

Harriet Wadsworth Tallmadge (1797–1856) married John Delafield Jr., the son of John (founder of New York University) and Mary Roberts Delafield, of New York City, on November 28, 1821. The couple had four children.[185]

George Washington Tallmadge (1803–1835) married Laura, daughter of Cahan Pease, of Warren, Ohio, on September 13, 1824. He lived in Tallmadge, Ohio, where he died in 1835. His widow married V.R. Humphrey, of Hudson, Ohio.

FREDERICK SAMUEL TALLMADGE

President of the Sons of the Revolution from 1884 to 1904, Frederick Samuel Tallmadge was the grandson of Colonel Benjamin Tallmadge and the great-grandson of Signer Colonel William Floyd, of Long Island. He was the son of Frederick Augustus and Elizabeth Tallmadge. Born on January 24, 1824, in New York City, Frederick graduated from Columbia University in 1845. As an attorney and member of the firm Tracy, Tallmadge and Noyes, he never lost his love for history, which was sewn so deeply by his family roots. While he was active in many societies and clubs, such as the Cincinnati Society and the New York Historical Society, none struck a chord like his treasured affiliation with the Society of the Sons of the Revolution (SRNY).

OF TALLMADGE QUALITIES

At the funeral of Benjamin Tallmadge (II), Reverend Laurens P. Hickok, pastor of his church, spoke of him as one whose "influence had already reached his posterity, and whose name will long live in the records of his country's history, and in the cherished remembrance of coming generations of children."[186] Reverend Hickok's words would ring true. As a very humble man, while the Tallmadge mystique of today—created by the renewed interest in the Culper Ring through publications and even video games—might have intrigued him, few historians believe he would have considered it in good taste.

Chapter 15

THE TRUMBULL FAMILY OF LEBANON

A s England endeavored to make peace with Holland, France and Spain,
Governor Jonathan Trumbull peered out a window from his Lebanon
War Office, well aware that the all-too-familiar view of his New London
County landscape would soon change forever.

It had been well over a year since the surrender of Cornwallis at
Yorktown, and the months of uncertainty had created a pronounced level of
consternation. As a seasoned leader, Trumbull sensed it from every direction.
The concern, and it was as cogent as it was complex, was the structure of a
new nation and its nascent states. This fine line, drawn between federalism
and states' rights, could make or break a republic or, for that matter, a political
career. Trumbull's opinions, which included an undeterred view in favor of
a strong central government and the abolition of the states' wage and price
controls, had nearly cost him an election—it did cost him the popular vote in
the May 1783 ballot, but as before, the General Assembly, forever confident
in his leadership, elected him to the governorship. It would, however, be his
final term of public service.

If anxiety or remorse had ever played any role in the life of this
indefatigable leader, it was never for public consumption; he had not, as he
so vehemently believed, lost a daughter, a son and a spouse in vain.

Inside the Lebanon War Office, a place many consider the early epicenter of the American Revolution.

Faith in Family

Jonathan Trumbull, a successful mercantilist turned politician, married seventeen-year-old Faith Robinson, of Duxbury, Massachusetts, on December 9, 1735. Faith, born on December 13, 1718, was the daughter of the Reverend John and Hannah (Wiswall) Robinson of Duxbury. The beautiful teenager bore a kind resemblance to her mother, whom she had tragically lost (aboard a small vessel making passage from Duxbury to Boston, Faith's mother, along with her eldest sister, Mary, drowned at Nantasket Beach). The four-year-old youth was then left to assist her eccentric father and three elder sisters.

As *Mayflower* stock, the Robinsons were a prominent New England family. The daughter of pilgrims John and Priscilla (Mullins) Alden, Elizabeth married William Pabodie of Duxbury on December 26, 1644. Their daughter Priscilla married Reverend Ichabod Wiswall, also of Duxbury, on December 10, 1679. And it was their daughter Hannah who married Reverend John Robinson, Faith's father.[187]

A forceful yet loving father, along with her siblings, is from whom Faith drew her spirit. Making habit of visiting her sister Mrs. Eliot—wife of Reverend Jacob Eliot, the pastor of Goshen parish in Lebanon—proved fruitful one day when she met the striking figure of Jonathan Trumbull. Although others claim the meeting was a business visit by Trumbull to Duxbury, the outcome remained the same: love.

When a salary dispute drove Reverend Robinson from Duxbury, he, too, turned to Lebanon. Located in the Windham Region of eastern Connecticut, it was the home to two of his married daughters. Reverend Robinson died in the town on November 14, 1745, at the age of seventy-four.

OF THE CHILDREN

Marriage soon brought Jonathan and Faith a family of six.[188] The combination—two sons followed by two daughters followed by two more sons—would prove nothing short of impressive.

The eldest son, Joseph (1737–1778), graduated from Harvard (1756) and then spent eleven years engaged in his father's mercantile business. He would then serve in the Twelfth Connecticut as a captain before being sent to the state's General Assembly. Stepping forward to answer Washington's call for assistance, he was appointed as the first commissary general of stores and provisions for the army of the United Colonies on July 19, 1775, a near impossible task, considering the lack of reliable suppliers and available currency. Yet Joseph, an experienced international trader, was relentless in his business duties, even at the expense of his health. The safe transportation of war supplies, often purchased on nothing more than promises, eventually overwhelmed the young man, his death attributed to the "perpetual cares and fatigues" of his office.[189] He would leave behind a wife, Amelia Dyer, daughter of Eliphalet Dyer, of Windham.[190] The blow would strike hard and deep to the soul of both Jonathan and Faith. What little consolation that could be found was in the arms of each other. Joseph, no less heroic than the soldier who had perished in battle, had also fallen for the cause of freedom.

Jonathan Trumbull Jr. (1740–1809) was also a Harvard College graduate (1759). He married Eunice Backus, daughter of Ebenezer and Eunice (Dyer) Backus, of Norwich, on March 26, 1767, and together they had one son and four daughters. Taking the staircase to public service, one solid step at a time, Trumbull began in the state legislature, serving multiple terms (1774–75, 1779–80, 1788), including as Speaker of the House in 1788. From July 28, 1775, until the death of his brother in 1778, Trumbull honored the office of deputy paymaster general for the Northern Department of the Continental army. He was then appointed comptroller of the treasury (1778–79) of the United States—a top-level placement under Roger Sherman's organization—before his installation as secretary and aide-de-camp to General George Washington in 1781.

A return to public service included Trumbull's attendance at the first three congresses (1789–95) before becoming lieutenant governor of Connecticut under Oliver Wolcott. Ascending to the governorship following Wolcott's death in office, Trumbull Jr. was reelected for an astounding eleven consecutive terms, serving from 1797 until his death. He was interred in the East Cemetery, near his father.[191]

A third son, David, was born on February 5, 1752.[192] Without his brothers, he was Faith's shoulder. Household tasks, and there were many, fell under his guidance. The father, too, turned to the son, as David would deliver dispatches and even oversee the transportation of provisions. Taking a fancy to firearms, David saw to both the acquisition of parts and equipment repair. And when assistance was needed from both the commissary and quartermaster's departments, he answered.

On December 6, 1778, David Trumbull married Sarah Backus, also a daughter of Ebenezer and Eunice (Dyer) Backus of Norwich. Together they had six children, one of whom died immediately after birth. From being a successful farmer to serving his neighbors in the General Assembly, David's heart was never far from Lebanon. He passed on January 17, 1822; his wife followed on June 2, 1846.

Youngest son John, the artist, was born on June 6, 1756. Although a childhood accident contributed to blindness in one eye, it was soon obvious that nothing was going to encumber his ambitions. Also a Harvard graduate, he served in the Continental army—early in the Revolution as an aide to General Washington—before it became clear that he preferred a brush over a bayonet. Trumbull resigned his commission in 1777. In 1780, under advisement from a friend, he went to London to study under painter

The exterior of the Lebanon, Connecticut home of Governor Jonathan Trumbull. *Library of Congress*.

Benjamin West. Unfortunately, it was a very volatile period, and he was imprisoned on suspicion of treason and eventually deported. Unfettered, Trumbull returned to London four years later, where, at the suggestion of West and with the encouragement of Thomas Jefferson, he began his famous national history work.

After the war, John's father urged him to take up the study and practice of law. Skeptical of his son's pursuit of art, he reminded John, "Connecticut is not Athens." (The reference a contrast between the state and one of the most important fifth-century BC cultural centers.) John's great-great-grandson of the same name later wrote, "He [Jonathan] never again attempts to influence the choice of his [John's] career."[193]

On October 1, 1800, John Trumbull married Sarah Hope Harvey, an English amateur painter. Finally settling in New York City, John secured a commission from Congress in 1816 to decorate the Capitol Rotunda. His works *Declaration of Independence*, *Surrender of General Burgoyne*, *Surrender of Lord Cornwallis* and *General George Washington Resigning His Commission* would become his hallmarks, chiefly for their documentary value. On November 10, 1843, he would pass on at the age of eighty-seven.

Faith (1743–1775), the eldest daughter, had a passion for art and would even inspire her youngest brother (John would later recall marveling over her tapestries that hung in their mother's parlor). Faith was sent to a boarding school in Boston (formal education for girls was considered a luxury at that time), where she was taught reading, writing, arithmetic and classical languages along with art. On May 1, 1766, she married the handsome and commanding Jedidiah Huntington of Norwich. Three years later, the young man would begin what would be a very illustrious military career—rising from ensign of the First Norwich Company to brigadier general of the Continental army (May 1777), Huntington was brevetted as major general by the war's end.

It was while visiting Boston with friends, at the time of the Battle of Bunker Hill, that Faith witnessed firsthand the cruelties of battle. Awaiting her husband, whose regiment was en route, the chaos with its frightening sounds and horrific images enveloped her being. In what might have been anxiety or something far more complex, she lingered in a state of unpredictable behavior. On November 24, 1775, she took her own life. Jonathan Trumbull, in a letter dated February 26, 1776, stated to his son-in-law: "The world, after all, is a little pitiful thing, not performing any one promise it makes us, and every day taking away and annulling the joys of the past."[194]

The governor's fourth child and youngest daughter was Mary (1745–1831), who caught the attention of William Williams, a resolute Patriot and a signer of the Declaration of Independence.

THE WILLIAMS BRANCH

Born in Lebanon on April 8, 1731, to Pastor Solomon and Mary Porter Williams, William was educated at Harvard before starting theological studies with his father. Like many, the French and Indian War interrupted William's career aspirations, and he soon found himself on the staff of his uncle Colonel Ephraim Williams, commander of the frontier posts west of the Connecticut River.[195] When the colonel was ambushed and killed at Lake George, New York, it had a profound effect on William.

Returning to Lebanon, William Williams became a merchant and was

elected town clerk, an office he held for over four decades. Resolved to public service, he held a variety of local and state positions and even attracted the attention of the governor's daughter. On February 14, 1771, a more mature Williams married Mary Trumbull, and the couple had three children: Solomon (II); Faith, who married John McClellan; and William (II), who married his cousin Sarah Trumbull.

The steeple of the First Congregational Church, located on the Green in Lebanon, Connecticut. It is the only surviving example of John Trumbull's architectural work.

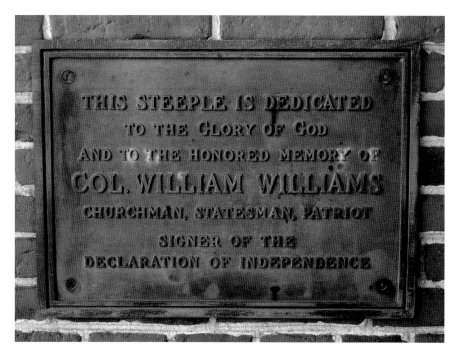

This plaque adorns the First Congregational Church and is dedicated to the memory of Colonel William Williams.

In 1776, the Connecticut Assembly appointed Williams a delegate to the Continental Congress, replacing Oliver Wolcott, who had taken ill. While his appointment enabled him to sign the Declaration, Williams never took part in its debate nor cast a vote for the illustrious document.

Known for his progressive views on politics and religion, Williams was not one who would simply blend into the walls, so to speak, of Lebanon's Alden Tavern. Instead, he would profess his views with little provocation, and often with great patriotic zeal.

Solomon (II), the couple's eldest son, died in 1810. Neither parent would fully recover from the loss. Health failing, the old Patriot passed away on August 2, 1811. Mary died nearly two decades later, on February 9, 1831. Both were interred in the Trumbull Family Cemetery.

FAITH ROBINSON

Not a cloud from the Revolution could remove Faith Robinson Trumbull from her post. She was a devoted mother, ever so quick to aid in a stressful situation. When her brave sons stepped forward to answer the call to arms, she did not balk or shed a tear of hopelessness. Instead, she would provide inspiring farewells, cognizant that a family, not an individual, had answered the call to arms.

To Jonathan, she was a rock—ever so solid and persevering. Through forty-five years of married life, their journey took them down a formidable path incomprehensible to most, especially during the eighteenth century. As for the children, they were all devoted, educated and of an independent mind and spirit, thanks to her assiduity.

The Trumbulls were active in their daily life and provided a secure support system for friends and relatives—Jonathan as a strong spiritual advisor and Faith as a spouse beyond reproach. To this day, it is not difficult to picture the pair walking hand in hand along the prodigious Lebanon Green, sharing a few moments of tranquility.

PASSING THE TORCH

As the American Revolution drew to a close, Connecticut conversation shifted from battlefield specifics to those who once orchestrated the struggle. "Half-pay," or the allowance an officer received after retirement, became the concern of the day. Opposition to the granting of such payment for life to retiring officers—or any compromise, for that matter—was felt strongest in Connecticut. In a democratic society, state leaders felt that there was no favored class, no element of aristocracy. Nor, in their minds, would there be a need for a fraternal order or brotherhood to commemorate those of army rank. The Society of the Cincinnati would prove to only fuel their consternation (the governor's son Jonathan was a charter member and was followed by his brother John). The governor, who did not bear a continental commission, willfully accepted the first honorary membership.[196] To some, however, the Trumbull family's involvement was a clear sign of their passion for federalism.

During the October 1783 session of the Connecticut General Assembly, and only days before his seventy-third birthday, Governor Trumbull delivered his farewell address. A man who, for more than a half century, had had the confidence of the people was now growing tired of the apprehensions that came along with his position and the infirmities of old age. In typical Trumbull fashion, his remarks were firm, direct and without remorse. He closed the address with: "Finally, my fellow-citizens, I exhort you to love one another: let each study the good of his neighbor and of the community, as his own. Hate strifes, contentions, jealousies, envy, avarice, and every evil work, and ground yourselves in this faithful and sure axiom, that virtue exalteth a nation, but that sin and evil workings are the destruction of a people."[197]

The response to Trumbull's statement was a resolution of sincere gratitude "[for his] display of wisdom, justice, fortitude and magnamity."[198] And this while the majority remained unwilling to endorse his political views.

A LEBANON RETIREMENT

In August 1785, after having spent over a year of retirement in the tranquility of his hometown, Trumbull developed a fever that overcame his body. For a dozen days, he fought and resisted its effects until at last, on the seventeenth

The Trumbull family burial plot at Lebanon's Old Cemetery.

of August, he could resist no more. His son Jonathan recorded the event in the family Bible, noting that his father's death was "easy, quiet and clam" and that he was "in possession of Reason to the last, as far as could be discovered."[199]

As a testimonial to his life, perhaps the words of George Washington account for it best:

> *A long and well-spent life in the service of his country places Governor Trumbull among the first of patriots. In the social duties he yielded to no one; and his lamp, from the common course of nature, being nearly extinguished, worn down with age and cares, yet retaining his mental faculties in perfection, are blessings which rarely attend advanced life. All these combined, have secured to his memory unusual respect and love here, and, no doubt, unmeasurable* [sic] *happiness hereafter.*[200]

Chapter 16

THE WEBSTER FAMILY OF WEST HARTFORD AND NEW HAVEN

The foundation of all free government and all social order must be laid in families and in the discipline of youth. Young persons must not only be furnished with knowledge, but they must be accustomed to subordination and subjected to the authority and influence of good principles. It will avail little that youths are made to understand truth and correct principles, unless they are accustomed to submit to be governed by them…And any system of education…which limits instruction to the arts and sciences, and rejects the aids of religion in forming the character of citizens, is essentially defective.
—Noah Webster[201]

THE LIFE OF JOHN WEBSTER

John Webster, baptized on August 16, 1590, in Cossington, Leicestershire, England, was the son of Matthew and Elizabeth (Ashton) Webster. With a lineage of some substance, he took the hand of Agnes Smith on November 7, 1609, in Cossington. The couple had a large family and, despite what appears to have been a comfortable life, set out for the New World. Settling first in Watertown, Massachusetts, they headed to Hartford, likely as part of Thomas Hooker's band, which departed Newtown in April 1636.

Lexicographer Noah Webster (1758–1843), the "Schoolmaster of the Republic." *Library of Congress.*

Webster immediately became involved in the settlement, holding offices such as assistant in the General Court of the Colony of Connecticut, commissioner to the United Colonies of New England and deputy governor of the Colony of Connecticut. Proving invaluable to the community, he was elected by the Colony of Connecticut as deputy governor in 1655, with Thomas Welles as governor. Since it was believed that no person should serve a term of more than one year, Webster was elected governor the following year.

The Reverend Thomas Hooker, who founded the Colony of Connecticut and headed the First Congregational Church, died in 1647. The difficult choice of his successor created both a political and spiritual crisis, as the separation of church and state did not yet exist. While the majority choice was Reverend Samuel Stone, Hooker's assistant, the minority favored Michael Wigglesworth. John Webster, one of the leading members of the First Congregational Church of Hartford, also supported the dissenting group. The complex conflict was eventually solved by the Connecticut legislature in May 1669 and was known as the Half-Way Covenant. By that time, the Hadley Company, as the dissenting group was known, was determined to leave Hartford with John Webster as one of its leaders. Their first destination of choice was Northhampton, Massachusetts, followed later by Hadley, Massachusetts, where John was made a magistrate in May 1660. A fever took John Webster's life on April 5, 1661, and six years later, his wife, Agnes, died in Hartford. John and Agnes Webster were Noah Webster's great-great-great grandparents.

WORDS ABOUT NOAH

Noah Webster Jr., the "Father of American Scholarship and Education," was born on October 16, 1758, in West Hartford, Connecticut. The scion of Noah Webster Sr. (1722–1813) and Mercy Steele, he and his siblings—brothers Abraham (1751–1831) and Charles (born 1762) and sisters Mercy (1749–1820) and Jerusha (1756–1831)—were descendants of Governor William Bradford of Plymouth Colony through their mother's lineage.[202]

To support his family, Noah's father farmed and served as justice of the peace and deacon of the local Congregational church. He was also a militia captain. Like many West Hartford youngsters, Noah studied under the guidance of Reverend Nathan Perkins, minister of the West Division's Congregational Church, who was instrumental in preparing 150 young men for college. And Perkins's instruction paid dividends, as Noah entered Yale in September 1774 and graduated in September 1778. However, life in New Haven wasn't so simple then, as the near constant threat of a British assault loomed ominously over the institution. Beginning in March 1777 and ending in June 1778, some Yale classes were diverted to Farmington, Glastonbury and Wethersfield as a precaution.[203] Even though Noah's education was briefly interrupted by the militia—his service cut short by a student exemption—he saw no action. [204]

Among Webster's noteworthy Yale classmates were the ardent Jeffersonian Joel Barlow, Signer Oliver Wolcott and preacher Zephaniah Smith.[205] The young man even managed his way into the diary of Reverend Ezra Stiles, soon to become president of Yale College, who noted Webster's dispute over a literary selection.

Upon graduation, Noah Webster found the times a bit discouraging. While his plan was to study law, he had little choice but to sustain himself, and this meant teaching at a school in Glastonbury in 1778.

The following year found him instructing in Hartford—a short distance from Glastonbury—and living with the family of future chief justice Oliver Ellsworth.

A northwest migration—no doubt at the urging of Ellsworth—soon found Webster in the town of Litchfield, Connecticut, where he either assisted Jedediah Strong, register of deeds, or perhaps worked with noted legal scholar Tapping Reeve. What is explicit is his admission to the bar in Hartford on April 3, 1781.[206]

But an enthusiastic Esquire Webster had trouble finding work. Again he turned to education, but this time as the founder of his own school in the northwest corner of the state. In a thought-provoking advertisement for his venture, he stated:

> On the first of May will be opened, at Sharon in Connecticut, a school, in which children may be instructed not only in the common arts of reading, writing, and arithmetic, but in any branch of academical literature. The little regard that is paid to the literary improvement of females, even among people of rank and fortune, and the general inattention to the grammatical purity and elegance of our native language, are faults in the education of the youth that more gentlemen have taken pains to censure than correct.[207]

With the price of board and tuition set at six to nine shillings' lawful money per week—age and study dependent—the young educator charted his course. An immediate success, the school attracted the children of many affluent families who had fled to Sharon following the British occupation of New York. However, Noah's ship was thrown off course. Instead of facing the provocations of affluence—which might have been easier, considering the circumstance—Webster faced the attraction and then rejection of a young woman, Rebecca Pordee of Sharon. The school soon closed without explanation.[208]

"In the year 1782, while the American army was lying on the bank of the Hudson, I kept a classical school in Goshen, Orange County, State of New York. I there compiled two small elementary books for teaching the English language. The country was then impoverished, intercourse with Great Britain was interrupted, school-books were scarce and hardly attainable, and there was no certain prospect of peace," Webster would write.[209] From Goshen, Webster would pen a spelling book (dissatisfied with the use of Dilworth's *New Guide to the English Tongue*, he felt it was time to separate not only our

The West Hartford home of Noah Webster. *Library of Congress.*

nation's philosophy from England but also our language) that would forever change his life.

Returning to Hartford, in the spring of 1783, Webster practiced law and wrote. In October 1783, he published his *American Spelling Book*, the famed "Blue-backed Speller," which was the first in the series of three volumes under the title *A Grammatical Institute of the English Language*. The work also persuaded him to conduct an active campaign in favor of copyright laws, a crusade Connecticut also embraced with prompt legislation. *Sketches of American Policy*, published on March 9, 1785, was a forty-eight-page manifest describing Webster's ideas on American nationalism. The publication, he believed, provided a solution to the type of education needed to achieve this new democracy. Not only would it be a prolific period in the author's life, but it was also one in which Webster established some priceless political contacts. During his extensive travels, from New Haven to South Carolina, he peddled his publications among such luminaries as George Washington, Thomas Paine and Benjamin Franklin.

From Hartford, Webster moved to Philadelphia (1786) and then on to New York (1787). In October 1788, he wrote in his diary an evaluation of his thirty years gone by: "I have read much, written much, and tried to do much good…and want the happiness of a friend whose interests and feelings should be mine." It appears that loneliness led him back to Hartford in May 1789.

THE FAMILY OF NOAH WEBSTER

Enter one charming lady from Boston, Rebecca "Becca" Greenleaf (1766–1847)—eight years younger than Noah. Following a romantic two-year courtship, the pair married on October 26, 1789, in New Haven. While keeping his eyes on family matters, Webster practiced law in Hartford until 1793, when he moved back to New York. He had founded two newspapers there—*American Minerva*, said to be the city's first daily newspaper, and the *Herald*—both of which were sold in 1803. Then, in 1798, Webster moved the family to New Haven, where he became active in local politics.

The couple had eight children. Emily (1790–1861) married William W. Ellsworth (1791–1868), a representative and Connecticut governor, and they had six children. Frances (1793–1869) married Chauncey Allen Goodrich, who became professor of rhetoric and English literature at Yale College. The Goodrichs had four children. Harriet (1797–1844) married William Chauncey Fowler, while Mary (1799–1819) married Horatio Southgate, a lawyer from Portland, Maine, and a nephew of Rufus King.[210] William (1801–1869) married Rosalie Eugenia Stuart. The couple had four children, including two sons who fought on opposing sides during the Civil War. The Confederate died in battle, while the other died of fever. When the couple divorced, William married Sarah Joanna Appleton. Eliza (1803–1888) married educator Henry Jones. The last-born children were Henry (1806–1807) and Louisa (1808–1874).[211]

Regarding the fastidiousness of the Webster women, Horatio Southgate might have reflected it best in a letter following the tragic death of his wife: "With such perfect good did she attend to every duty, that it would seem to her she had done nothing, and yet so great was her fidelity in every branch of domestic life as to leave nothing to be done."[212]

Noah loved Becca and the children dearly, as evidenced by his correspondence, but his anachronistic views on women—which were not uncommon for the time—contradicted his own beliefs. For example, "No man ever marries a woman for her performance on a harpsichord, or her

The interior of a room at the Noah Webster House in West Hartford. *Library of Congress.*

figure in a minuet. However ambitious a woman may be to command admiration abroad, her real merit is known only at home. Admiration is useless when it is not supported by domestic worth."[213] For someone who abhorred the autocratic power displayed by the British, these comments were a bit out of character.

ON TO AMHERST

Successful beyond imagination, Webster's publications provoked praise and adoption—his dialect became our language. His *Compendious Dictionary of the English Language* was published in 1806, clearing the way for his 1828 landmark, *An American Dictionary of the English Language*, which contained over seventy thousand entries and was published in two volumes.[214] The Webster family moved from New Haven to Amherst, Massachusetts, in 1812, and helped to found the Amherst Collegiate Institute, later Amherst College. Living in a house on Main Street, facing the Common, Noah supported his family through farming and publishing income; he also served in the Massachusetts legislature and continued working on his dictionary. The family moved back to New Haven in 1822. Noah died there on May 28, 1843. After suffering for nearly a year from the effects of a paralytic stroke, Rebecca "Becca" Greenleaf died on July 25, 1847.

As for his political association, Webster defended, through his New York newspapers, both George Washington and John Adams. Such an action was expected from a Federalist spokesman. However, he declined the request to tutor Washington's stepchildren because it would require his full attention and detract from writing, his "principal pleasure."[215] Later, during a capital dinner, Webster criticized President Andrew Jackson for the amount of foreign food and wine he served. Naturally, he thought it would be far more patriotic (his nationalist sentiment was resolute) to serve American fare.[216]

A bit arrogant at times and even a curmudgeon of sorts, Noah Webster once envisioned that his work—his patois of nationalism—had contributed to not only the nation's youth but also the sovereign state as a whole. That dream came true.

Chapter 17

THE WOLCOTT FAMILY OF
WINDSOR AND LITCHFIELD

Every Thing is leading to the lasting Independancy of these Colonies.
—Oliver Wolcott, June 1776

O liver Wolcott, who entered the world on November 20, 1726, in Windsor, Connecticut, was the enterprising son of Roger Wolcott (1679–1767) and Sarah (Drake) Wolcott (1684–1748).[217] Graduating from Yale in 1747, he accepted a captain's commission from New York governor George Clinton and served in the defense of the northern frontier during King George's War (the third of the four French and Indian Wars, 1744–48). When the war ended, Wolcott returned home to study medicine with his brother, Dr. Alexander Wolcott.[218] While it was Oliver's intent to set up a practice in Goshen, he changed his mind.

By 1751, the relatively new town of Litchfield, where his father had purchased a parcel of land, attracted Oliver's attention. That year, he became the town's first sheriff, a position he held for twenty years, and pondered an entrance into politics. But before too many steps could be taken, he took the hand of Lorraine (Laura) Collins on January 21, 1755.

As the daughter of Daniel and Lois (Cornwall) Collins of Guilford, Laura was blessed with intellectual acuity complemented by elegance. An attractive and well-mannered woman who had been given the opportunity to pursue a business career would have no doubt been successful—not a surprise, considering her lineage, which included Governor William Leete. According to author George Gibbs, "She [Laura] possessed a degree of

Opposite: A statue of Oliver Wolcott adorns the exterior of the Hartford State Capitol.

Above: The symmetrical Georgian-style home of Oliver Wolcott Sr.

courage remarkable even in those days of female heroism, and a masculine judgment and business character which seconded effectually her husband's pursuits, while they lightened their burden."[219] The couple would have five children, and the four who survived infancy were welcome hands on the family farm, a supplement to Oliver's civil offices.

From a town representative in the General Assembly to councilor and even a judge, if Oliver Wolcott could assist the district of Litchfield, he most certainly would. This commitment also held true for the militia, where he served in every grade from captain to major general.

Oliver Wolcott was elected as a delegate to the Continental Congress in 1775, and except for 1779, when he was not chosen, served religiously until 1783. As a Signer, he approved the adoption of the Declaration of Independence and was steadfast in his pursuit of freedom.

True to form, when the war broke out, Wolcott contributed where needed: as a member of the state council (1774–86), as judge of the county court of common pleas and as judge of probate for the Litchfield District. During the summer of 1775, he was named one of the commissioners of Indian affairs for the Northern Department. Settling the Wyoming Valley (northeastern Pennsylvania) and the New York–Vermont boundary issues while inducing the Indians to remain neutral was no simple task and required Wolcott to meet with the representatives of the Six Nations: the Tuscarora and Oneida, who sided with the colonists, and the Mohawk, Seneca, Onondaga and Cayuga, who remained loyal to Great Britain.

His efficiency as a leader in the Connecticut militia proved invaluable during the American Revolution. Later, his emphasis would shift to the coastal defenses of the state before accepting a valuable position with the Council of Safety.

As the war drew to a conclusion, Wolcott turned back to his home in Litchfield. He resigned from Congress, not out of disinterest for public service—he served as commissioner at the Treaty of Fort Stanwix in 1784 to make peace with the Six Nations—but out of a need to spend more time with his family. Since Hartford was far closer than New York City or Philadelphia, he thought that perhaps a local office would suffice. He served as lieutenant governor of Connecticut from 1786 until 1796 before becoming governor.

THE FAMILY

While four decades of marriage brought the couple much satisfaction, it was not without sacrifice. At home, Laura saw to the needs of both her community and family. She was quick to extend a helping hand to neighbors or to donate her time in support of a patriotic or religious effort. As Congregationalists and devout Christians, faith-based expectations needed to be fulfilled, and she saw to those as well. From the Wolcott farmstead also came provisions—blankets from their hands, victuals from their soil.

A woman of considerable strength, both in mind and spirit, Laura was the stalwart of the family. In her husband's absence, she attended to the family farm, managed its finances (brilliantly, according to many) and saw to the education of their children.[220] If distributing parental love and attention were not hard enough for one parent, try doing it for two. Laura's love was divided among Oliver Wolcott (I), who died young; Oliver Wolcott Jr. (1760–1833), who would marry Elizabeth (Betsy) Stoughton on June 1, 1785; Laura (1761–1814), who would marry William Moseley on October 6, 1785; Mariann (1765–1805), who would marry Chauncey Goodrich in 1789; and finally Frederick (1767–1837), who first married Betsey Huntington on October 12, 1800, and then Sally Cooke on June 21, 1815.

In available portraits, Laura Wolcott Moseley appears the perfect mix between her parents—the long countenance of the Wolcotts complemented flawlessly by the Collins beauty. Her son and only child, Charles Moseley, would turn to the legal profession like his father. Graduating from both Yale and the Litchfield Law School, he would establish a legal practice in Hartford. Charles never married and died at the young age of twenty-eight.

The amiable Mariann Wolcott Goodrich and her husband, Chauncey, lived in Connecticut early in their marriage. While he practiced law and served in the state's house of representatives, Mariann visited family and mingled at social gatherings. Chauncey, who would become a seasoned politician, served numerous terms as a state representative (1795–1801) and later as a senator (1807–13). He and his gregarious and sharp-witted wife quickly established themselves in the societal circles of New York, Philadelphia and Washington, D.C. Having never had children allowed them the luxury of doting on their siblings, nieces and nephews. Chauncey's sister married Henry Leavitt Ellsworth, son of Chief Justice Oliver Ellsworth, and his nephew, Chauncey Allen Goodrich, was the son-in-law of wordsmith Noah Webster.[221] Regrettably, Mariann Goodrich died at the young age of forty.

Graduating from Yale in 1786, Frederick Wolcott received his degree from Litchfield Law School the following year. While illness prevented him from practicing law, it did little to curtail his public ambitions. Frederick served his community as clerk of the Court of Common Pleas (1793–1836), judge of probate (1796–1836) and clerk of the Superior Court of the County (1798–1836), while also handling the tasks of state representative (1802–03) and state senator (1810–23). Frederick and his first wife had four daughters and two sons, while he and his second spouse had two daughters. He died in Litchfield, Connecticut, at the age of sixty-nine.

OLIVER WOLCOTT JR.

As the eldest son, much was expected from Oliver Jr. And much was indeed delivered. His mother's attention, as apportioned as it was, seemed more direct with young Oliver as she tutored him early in preparation for grammar school. Later, her instruction proved fruitful, as Oliver entered Yale College at the age of thirteen and graduated in 1778. Afterward, he returned home

Built by Elijah Wadsworth, this house was purchased by Oliver Wolcott Jr. in 1814, when he moved back to Litchfield from New York City.

to attend the Litchfield Law School, where the eminent Tapping Reeve, well aware of the Wolcott name, then saw to the youth's instruction.

During the Revolution, Oliver served as his father's aide-de-camp and then as quartermaster (1779–1881). Admitted to the bar in 1781, he left the army with hopes of practicing law but instead turned to the financial sector, working in Hartford as a member of the Committee of the Pay Table (1782–88), which became the Office of the Comptroller of Public Accounts in 1788, with Oliver fittingly serving as the first comptroller.

In 1789, Oliver became the first auditor of the federal treasury, and two years later he was appointed comptroller of the Treasury Department. In 1795, following the resignation of Alexander Hamilton, he began his service as secretary of the treasury under President George Washington (1795–1800). After serving in this capacity until November 1800—following accusations of improprieties by political enemies, Wolcott left the cabinet—and after a short period as judge for the Second Circuit Court (1801–02), he retired from public service.

In 1803, Oliver moved with his family to New York, where he entered into a business partnership (known as Oliver Wolcott & Company) with James Watson, Moses Rogers, Archibald Gracie and William Woolsey. Following the firm's dissolution, Wolcott continued as a member of the board of directors for the Bank of the United States (1810–11) and established the Bank of America. He served as its president from 1812 through 1814.

Returning to Litchfield in 1815, his hopes for a quieter life quickly diminished when he was elected governor of Connecticut, a position he held for ten consecutive one-year terms through 1826. Under complex financial setbacks and emotional stress, Wolcott later returned to New York, where he lived with his daughter Laura Wolcott Gibbs and her husband, George Gibbs. Oliver Wolcott and Elizabeth Stoughton had had five sons (three of whom died in infancy) and two daughters. Wolcott died in New York City on June 1, 1833, and was the last surviving member of George Washington's cabinet.

A BIT OF ANCESTRY

Some believe that the Wolcott family can be traced back to the knight Sir John Wolcott in 1382, while others believe the first firm footing of the line in England to be William Wolcott (1463–1502). For certain, Henry Wolcott, from the Parish of Lyiard, St. Lawrence, Somersetshire, and his wife, Elizabeth Saunders, emigrated on the ship *Mary and John*.[222] Leaving behind (albeit temporarily) three children, one of whom would become Oliver's grandfather Siman, they departed Plymouth, England, and arrived in Massachusetts on May 31, 1630.[223]

Settling first in Dorchester, the Wolcott family then headed southwest to Windsor, Connecticut, six years later. Their new English settlement suited them just fine, and Henry soon found comfort in public service. He was a member of the first General Assembly of Connecticut (1637), the House of Delegates (1637–43) and the House of Magistrates (1643–55). Both Henry and his wife, Elizabeth, died in 1655 and were interred in the churchyard of the First Congregational Church in Windsor.

Oliver's grandfather Siman, having joined his family in or about 1640, also pursued public service. He married his second wife, Martha Pitkin (1639–1719), sister of William Pitkin, the attorney general and treasurer of

Connecticut, in 1661; Siman's first spouse, Joanna Cook (1625–1687), had died some time earlier. In 1667, Wolcott received a land grant at Simsbury, and four years later, he sold his Windsor property to pursue the endowment. Having served in the First Connecticut Cavalry (1658), he would add captain of the Simsbury militia to his credentials in 1673. This, however, was a very dangerous period, as King Phillip's War (1675–78) was being waged between the Native American inhabitants and English colonists (and their Native American allies). When Simsbury was reduced to ashes following an Indian raid, Oliver turned back to Windsor, considered a frontier village at the time. Settling on a large spread on the south side of the river, the Wolcotts were content again to resume their life. When Siman passed in 1687, the six children were left to the care of Martha. The youngest, Roger, born in 1679, was Oliver's father.

With a half dozen children to care for, Martha's time was at a premium, even if you were the youngest. Without a formal education, Roger turned to reading, especially books on the law. He also turned to Sarah Drake, whom he married in 1702. The couple had fifteen children, eight of whom would survive childhood.

Roger's political aspirations began in 1707 with his role as selectman for the town of Windsor. Two years later, he was admitted to the bar, and two years after that to the General Assembly. Considering everything he had endured, persistence seems to have become his hallmark. But the challenges the family would face were not over.

In 1711, Queen Anne's War (1702–13), the second in a series of French and Indian Wars fought between France and England, was still being waged. Sarah Drake Wolcott would then have to endure Roger's absence when he joined the militia as the supply master during the expedition to Quebec. He felt it not only Connecticut's obligation but also his own.

Roger's return after the war found him in the General Assembly (assistant, 1714–41) and in the courts (judge, Hartford County Court, 1721–32; judge, Connecticut Superior Court, 1732–41; and chief judge, Superior Court, 1741–50). Additionally, in 1741, he was elected deputy governor of the colony under Royal Governor Jonathan Law.

Opposite, top: The carved gravestone of Siman Wolcott as it appears in the Windsor family plot.

Opposite, bottom: The graves of Roger and Sarah Drake Wolcott are marked by this black table tomb in the Palisado Cemetery in Windsor.

And if that weren't enough, while serving as deputy governor in 1745, the sixty-seven-year-old major general was asked to command the Connecticut troops—second in command of all New England troops—in a United Colonies expedition against the French at Louisbourg on Cape Breton, Nova Scotia, Canada.[224] Tragically, he would have only a little time left with Sarah when he arrived home in 1747; she passed the following year at the age of sixty-three. For Oliver, fresh out of Yale, the year might have been the most meaningful of his life.

In 1750, upon the death of Governor Law, Oliver would witness his father become the next royal governor of the Colony of Connecticut, a position he would hold until 1754. At seventy-six years of age, Roger Wolcott was defeated in that year's election—a new event for Connecticut, as all previous governors had died in office. As content as any Wolcott ever was, he returned to the family farm. Roger Wolcott died on May 17, 1767, in Windsor and is buried in Palisado Cemetery.

42,088, BUT WHO'S COUNTING?

On the evening of July 9, 1776, Oliver Wolcott was in New York City when General George Washington read—there was an order to assemble promptly at six o'clock to hear an announcement approved by the Continental Congress calling for American independence from Great Britain—the Declaration of Independence to his troops. The words were so moving that the citizens who had heard the proclamation raced down Broadway toward a large four-thousand-pound equestrian statue of King George III and pulled it down. The crowd cheered as the statue, made of lead coated with a fine layer of gold leaf, was shattered into pieces. When the mass cut off the statue's head, severed the nose and mounted what remained of the crown on a spike outside a tavern, the clamor was deafening. Some even claim that the head of the statue was sent back to England as proof of insurrection.

But it would be Oliver Wolcott who would organize a more befitting crucifixion. He arranged for the fragments to be collected and shipped to the port of Norwalk, Connecticut. Upon arrival, the pieces were loaded onto oxcarts and rolled the sixty-some miles to the general's home in Litchfield. In a community event, Oliver and Laura gathered behind their house in an orchard and, together with some local patriotic women, melted

The grave marker of Oliver Wolcott (1726–1797) and Laura Collins Wolcott (1732–1794).

the lead and shaped it into bullets. The Wolcotts' own son, Frederick, would later attest that his father took an axe and chopped up some of the lead pieces himself. One can only imagine the sight of such a modest man engaging in such an action. In a memorandum purported to be in the handwriting of Oliver Wolcott himself and now in the possession of the Connecticut Historical Society, there is a list of the people who helped to make the 42,088 bullets.[225]

Chapter 18

THE WOOSTER FAMILY OF DERBY
AND NEW HAVEN

The grave of Wooster is no longer unmarked. No longer do his ashes slumber among a thankless people. The State to its child, its bulwark and martyr, Masonry to the master-builder of its oldest temple, and Danbury to its self-sacrificing avenger, have at length yielded the slow tribute of a monument.
—Representative Henry Champion Deming, Danbury, April 27, 1854[226]

These poignant remarks—part of an oration delivered by Deming at the dedication of a monument to the memory of David Wooster—provided closure to a community still grieving the loss of their hero nearly eight decades ago. "High in its commanding position, it now overlooks the commonwealth he served and the field on which he fell," Deming continued. "It proclaims to the South his devotion as a patriot, to the East his fidelity as a brother: the arms of the State with its God-trusting motto, and the emblems of military heroism, appropriately honor and embellish it: it stretches far up toward the heaven to which his faith aspired, and it is fittingly surmounted by the glorious bird which he helped make the symbol of victory, and the invincible standard-bearer of the Republic."[227]

Edward Wooster, David's grandfather, was one of the earliest settlers of Derby, an Indian trading post labeled Paugasset. At five square miles, this hamlet, named after Derby, England, in 1675, would become Connecticut's smallest municipality.

David's father had left Derby about 1706—nearly two decades before the town was incorporated—for Stratford, in the southeast corner of what is now Huntington, but returned when David was about ten or eleven years of age. It is believed (the family papers having been long since destroyed by the British when they pillaged New Haven in 1779) that the youth was reared in the Puritan principles of the era before graduating from Yale College in 1738.

The youngest of six children, David Wooster was born to Abraham and Mary Wooster on March 2, 1710, in Stratford (Huntington), Connecticut. Preceding David's arrival were Ruth (born 1700), Joseph (born 1702), Sarah (born 1705), Mary (born 1707) and Hannah (born 1709).[228]

WOOSTER AT SERVICE

Though it might not have been immediately evident as a youth, David Wooster had a gift for leadership and a growing passion for military service. As part of the British colonial militia (1739–45), he would participate in King George's War, including the Siege of Louisbourg (Canada). This conflict led to his service with the British army (1745–61), where he would play a role in the French and Indian War at the Battles of Carillon and Ticonderoga, and his legendary involvement with the Continental army (1775–77), which would include the Siege of Fort St. Jean (Quebec, Canada) and the tragic Battle of Ridgefield, Connecticut.

As a colonial militia lieutenant aboard the sloop *Defense*, the first war ship ever built for his native colony, Wooster initially spent time cruising between Cape Cod and the capes of Virginia—via inner passage through the Long Island Sound, keeping Connecticut shores safe from piratical invasion.[229] Promoted to captain—under a provincial regiment that was part of the troops sent by Connecticut under Colonel Andrew Burr, uncle to future vice president Aaron Burr—he quickly saw action at the Siege of Louisbourg (May 11–June 28, 1745). Seeing to the surrender of the Canadian fort, Wooster was then sent to France to negotiate the exchange of prisoners. Acknowledged in Great Britain for his exploits, he became a favorite of King George II, who presented him with a captain's baton in the regiment of Sir William Pepperell, along with a period of half pay.

The French and Indian War witnessed Wooster's promotion to the rank of colonel, his military acumen having earned him command of the Third Connecticut Regiment. And it was with this unit that he witnessed British

The Death of General Montgomery at Quebec, by John Trumbull. *Library of Congress.*

general James Abercrombie's now-classic example of military incompetence at Fort Carillon (July 6–8, 1758), later known as Fort Ticonderoga. (Over a year later, on July 26–27, 1759, General Jeffrey Amherst would correct the mishap and sustain occupation until the end of the conflict.)

When the Continental army was created, it needed to look no further than the spirited Wooster—among the eight brigadier generals appointed by the Congress on June 22, 1775, he would rank third. His troops became part of a long expedition—under the command of General Richard Montgomery, who was second in rank among the leadership—against Canada. This first major military initiative conducted by the Continental army found Wooster engaging at the Siege of Fort St. Jean (September 17–November 3, 1775), after which he took command of the fallen city of Montreal.

On December 31, 1775, at the age of thirty-seven, Sir Richard Montgomery was shot and killed during the ill-fated Battle of Quebec. The tragic loss of such a beloved general left an enormous void, but one that nevertheless needed to be filled. The arduous command would fall to Wooster, who soon found himself overwhelmed and even facing charges of incompetence over his tenure (at his request, a court-martial would later clear him).[230] Following a retreat back to Fort Ticonderoga, Wooster then returned to Connecticut.

At home in New Haven, Wooster was appointed major general of the state's militia. His defense during the winter of 1776–77 would center on the neighborhood of Danbury, where a significant amount of supplies had been collected. In April 1777, having just returned from a recent tour, Wooster was informed of an enemy landing (intent on the destruction of the precious Danbury magazines, a large body, quoted at roughly two thousand men, had arrived the previous day) between Norwalk and Fairfield at what is now Westport.

Wooster, having left orders for the militia to be mustered and dispatched immediately, set off for Fairfield to join forces with Brigadier General Gold S. Silliman. When inclement weather hampered his militia's punctual arrival, Wooster became concerned—would they reach Danbury in time to save it from destruction? Having overtaken Silliman's forces at Reading, Wooster took command and headed toward Bethel, where a decision was made to divide the troops. One part was sent off under Generals Arnold—who is said to have accompanied Wooster on his travel—and Silliman, while the other portion was to remain with Wooster. The goal was for the former to intercept the enemy—under the feared William Tryon—from the front while Wooster tormented from the rear. If the supplies could not be saved, he thought, then most certainly they could harass the British on their return to the coast.

By route of Danbury, Wooster overtook the enemy at about eleven o'clock the following morning near Ridgefield. Observing a small portion of enemy troops detaching themselves from the main body, he made the decision to attack. Outnumbered, the resolute commander led his inexperienced militia forward. However, with several field pieces at their disposal, the British quickly dispersed the assault. As the major general tried to renew the strike by rallying his collected troops, he was hit with a musket ball from behind. The shot broke his back. Having fallen from his horse, he was removed from the field, treated and conveyed by carriage to Danbury. There, at the Nehemiah Dibble mansion—where only hours before, the dreaded Tryon, who had conducted the enemy raid, had been headquartered—he was again given medical care. By the time Mary Wooster could reach her loving husband from New Haven, delirium had overtaken him, and he couldn't recognize her. David Wooster lived, inside the old South Street House, until May 2, 1777.

Less than two years before, in a letter dated July 7, 1775, to Roger Sherman, Wooster stated, "No man feels more sensibly for his distressed country, nor would more readily exert his utmost for its defence, than myself. My life has been ever devoted to the service of my country from youth up; though never before in a cause like this, a cause which I could most cheerfully risk, nay lay down my life to defend."

THE FAMILY OF DAVID WOOSTER

From every account, Mary Clap was healthy in both mind and spirit. She enjoyed the history and geography of New England and was never hesitant to share a delicious tidbit of information. Mary also delighted in the social element brought to her role as Mrs. David Wooster—there was prestige associated with being the consort of such a distinguished officer.

Regard was one thing, but consolation was another, and she found the latter in her love of the Gospel. Drawing strength from its essence, Mary lived the doctrine, giving to the poor and reaching out to the afflicted. And when the time came for her to deal with her own disappointments, she did so with remarkable courage. In the end, as her body fell prey to disease, her soul remained untarnished.

David Wooster (1710–1777) married Mary Clap (1729–1807), daughter of Yale president Reverend Thomas Clap and his wife, on March 6, 1745. She was sixteen years old. The couple would live at a homestead in New Haven and raise their four children. Mary (I) (1747–1748) and Mary (II) (1753–1754) died young. Thomas Wooster (1752–1792) served in the Revolutionary War and married Lydia Shelton, with whom he is believed to have had seven children. He perished on a voyage from New Orleans to New Haven. Mary Wooster (III) (born 1755) married Reverend John Cosens Ogden. The couple had three children, all of whom died unmarried.

Charles W. Wooster (1780–1848), the son of Thomas Wooster and grandson of General David Wooster, would aggressively carry the family sword.[231] Born at New Haven, Wooster went to sea at the young age of eleven and only a decade later was commanding the New York ship *Fair American* in trade to South America. As commander of the New York privateer brig *Saratoga* in the fall of 1812, he captured several vessels off the coast of Venezuela and quickly established himself as a fearless defender of his waters. Wooster also served as major of the New York Sea Fencibles, a naval militia that occupied the port's defenses during the War of 1812. Later, he served in the Chilean navy, retiring as admiral in 1829. He died

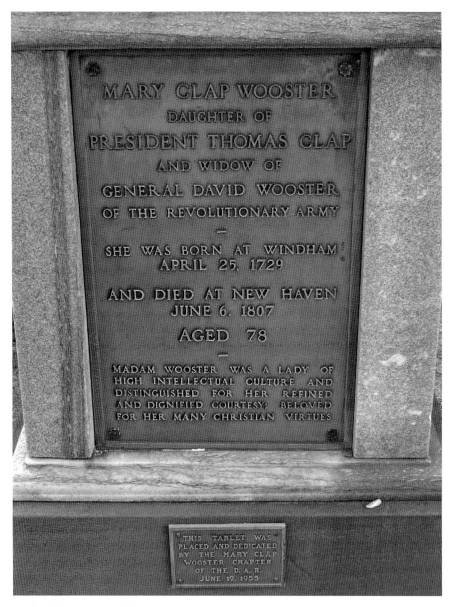

This tablet, dedicated to Mary Clap Wooster, is located at Grove Street Cemetery in New Haven.

in California in 1848. He had two sons, one of whom died in infancy. The second son, Charles F. Wooster, was educated at West Point and served in the Florida War and the war with Mexico. He died at Fort Brown, Texas, on February 14, 1856, at the young age of thirty-nine. It is through his spirit that four successive generations served their country.

Mary's husband, John Cosens Ogden, graduated from the College of New Jersey (Princeton University), one of the nine colonial colleges established before the American Revolution, and then moved to New Haven. Ordained a Protestant Episcopal priest in 1788, Ogden was unable to find permanent employment, so he traveled throughout Vermont and Canada confronting every religious, political and educational issue that came his way. In 1797, he published *An Appeal to the Candid Upon the Present State of Religion and Politics in Connecticut*, which ruffled a few feathers, before joining in the support of the outspoken Matthew Lyon, who had been arrested and imprisoned.[232] Ogden went so far as to gather petitions from many of Lyon's Vermont supporters and transport them to Philadelphia, where they were presented to John Adams. John Ogden died in Maryland in September 1800.[233]

The division created by the American Revolution was profound, splitting kinsfolk while uniting neighbors. And these were families who had not only had a colonial presence but also deep roots in the mother country. That bitterness, the struggle between Loyalists (Tories) and Patriots, also impacted David Wooster. For example, his uncle Thomas had eight children, including five—John, Henry, Thomas, Daniel and David—who were Tories.[234]

OF COURAGE AND ESTEEM

For centuries, the Wooster family name has exuded courage—obvious for the military exploits of David but less conspicuous for others. A perfect example is the dauntless comportment of Mary Clap. Two years after the death of her husband, on July 5, 1779, she faced a British raid on New Haven led by none other than Commander William Tryon. The aggressive leader—a man who long advocated attacks on civilian targets but had been thankfully held at bay by Sir Henry Clinton—targeted specifically the home of Mary Clap Wooster.

As British sentries stormed the Wooster home, destroying everything in their path—even casting her furniture into the street—this intransigent

A statue of David Wooster adorns the exterior of the Hartford State Capitol.

woman refused to leave her residence. Mary Clap Wooster would not be intimidated—not by her husband's executioners or anyone else. The enemy stole off with two trunks filled with family records; a few days later, whale boat captains would claim discovering an excess of related correspondence floating in area waters—the British fleet having been anchored off Fairfield. A seething Ezra Stiles, who was then president of Yale, admonished Tryon's tyrannical behavior and requested the correspondence (the lost papers included many of the early records of Yale College) returned, but none had apparently survived.

Tragically, without these records, Mary was unable to receive military compensation from the Continental Congress or the Assembly of Connecticut. Later, while living in poverty, she had to appeal to the legislature for assistance.[235] As is so often the case, the survivors of war often undergo the greatest pain.

Some have called David Wooster "a largely forgotten hero of the Revolution." His granddaughter, Mrs. Mary Clap Turner, viewed him in these words: "Large was his beauty and his soul sincere, calm and unruffled under great or minor public difficulties, of tall, fine, commanding personal appearance, those who knew him best have likened him to our beloved Washington."[236]

The Woosters, like other Connecticut families of the Revolution, command our utmost respect and appreciation. In nearly every Connecticut graveyard, we find "immortal examples of patriotic virtue, imperishable models of every exalted worth," as Henry Deming put it sixteen decades ago. And it hasn't changed since. The living seed of future heroes and Patriots was indeed in our fathers' dust.[237] These American forebears have endured through their words and through their actions. As our inspiration, and as our family, we are so very proud.

Notes

Chapter 1

1. The document was signed by the British treaty commissioner and the three American commissioners: Benjamin Franklin, John Adams and John Jay.
2. Western Massachusetts and Vermont were both settled by pioneers from Connecticut.
3. The churches, town meetings and schools were no longer strictly of the Puritan type, though that heritage was carefully preserved. Incoming missionaries provided a strong educational influence.
4. The first attack, in April, destroyed about twenty Patriot vessels and a sail loft, while the second saw the town face a three-day British bombardment.
5. Isaac Hull became a national hero aboard the frigate *Constitution*; Macdonough, who considered Middletown, Connecticut, his home, scored a victory at the Battle of Plattsburgh; William Hull, distinguished during the Revolution, surrendered command of the fort at Detroit to the British and faced a court-martial.
6. John Ledyard, of Groton, was the first Connecticut man to examine the potential of the Pacific Northwest. In 1776, he accompanied Captain James Cook on his third and last voyage around the world.

7. See Carol Karlsen's *The Devil in the Shape of a Woman* (1987) and John M. Taylor's *The Witchcraft Delusion in Colonial Connecticut, 1647–1697*.
8. In 1798, the general association of Congregational churches in the state of Connecticut organized itself as a missionary society.
9. Studies on the topic vary significantly due to the lack of accurate data.
10. On July 4, 1826, at the age of ninety, Adams lay on his deathbed while the country celebrated Independence Day. His last words were, "Thomas Jefferson still survives." He was mistaken: Jefferson had died five hours earlier at Monticello at the age of eighty-two.

CHAPTER 2

11. One noteworthy example is Robert F. Berkhofer Jr.'s *A Behavioral Approach to Historical Analysis* (New York: Free Press, 1969).
12. Root, *Chapter Sketches*, 57.
13. She also warned soldiers to prepare for a raid. Thanks to her daring actions, the British were halted at Ridgefield, Connecticut, on April 27, 1777, and forced to retreat to Long Island Sound.
14. Root, *Chapter Sketches*, 67.
15. Ibid., 71.
16. Ibid.
17. His name appears on the first Committee of Correspondence for the town of New London.
18. Salisbury, a town located in the most northwestern part of the state of Connecticut, was known for its valuable iron deposits.
19. Privateering generates a considerable amount of activity, including the adjudication of prize ships, exchange of prisoners and acquisition of cannon and powder for the government. All this activity required supervision, so the Continental Congress appointed a naval agent for each state.
20. When Washington came through New London after forcing the British evacuation of Boston in the spring of 1776, there was a grand assemblage of army and navy. Washington, Hopkins, General Nathanael Greene and other officers shared dinner at Nathaniel Shaw's house, where Washington was given the master bedroom for the night.
21. Root, *Chapter Sketches*, 98.

22. Ibid., 100.
23. Having been an area prone to self-defense, as a result of Indian conflicts, solace was slow in coming to the region.
24. Root, *Chapter Sketches*, 152.
25. Gold Silliman was the son of Ebenezer Silliman, a judge of the colony's Superior Court and a member of the governor's council. When Colonel Silliman took command of his regiment in March 1776, his dutiful son William also saw service.
26. Root, *Chapter Sketches*, 157.
27. Ibid., 159–61. She was pregnant with her son Benjamin at the time.
28. Ibid., 227.
29. The Litchfield Law School was founded in 1784, so this was under private instruction.

CHAPTER 3

30. A mischievous incident led to his dismissal from Yale.
31. Date recorded on grave marker; DAR states 1755.
32. This quote appears in many sources, including the Acton Institute's *Religion & Liberty* 21, no. 3 (Summer 2011).
33. Martin added the Greek Revival–style colonnaded porch to Elmwood in 1836.
34. Some sources say seven children; Martin and Sophia were married on October 19, 1807.
35. Joseph Hawley was Stratford's first town clerk, a tavern keeper and a shipbuilder.
36. On November 5, 1707, at the age of seventeen, Abiah Hawley, daughter of Ephraim and Sarah, took the hand of William Wolcott of East Windsor. "As rich as the Hawleys" was a Bridgeport aphorism.
37. "Nabby" was said to have looked strikingly similar to Oliver, thus the favoritism.
38. Connecticut's famed maple trees have replaced the original elms.
39. The Oliver Ellsworth Homestead is located at 778 Palisado Avenue in Windsor, Connecticut.
40. Ellsworth favored the three-fifths compromise on the enumeration of slaves but opposed the abolition of the foreign slave trade.

41. Oliver Ellsworth, Reference: *Essays on the Constitution of the United States,* Ford, ed. (146); original *The Connecticut Courant* [Sheehan (4:4)].

CHAPTER 4

42. The family was raised under a strict sect of New England Puritan orthodoxy.
43. Elizabeth, at the young age of forty, passed on April 21, 1767.
44. Johnston, *Nathan Hale*, 7.
45. This was not quite three months before Nathan entered college, leaving some question as to the intimacy of the relationship.
46. Alice Adams married Elijah Ripley. When he died, his eighteen-year-old widow returned to the Hale homestead with her infant son, who would pass only months later. Alice later married William Laurence.
47. Sarah died less than a year after her husband (1803).
48. Date of birth is listed in some sources as 1749.
49. Elizabeth (III), Rebeckah, Mary and Sarah.
50. Sources vary regarding Elizabeth's date of birth. Following the death of Dr. Samuel Rose, Elizabeth Rose married John Taylor of Coventry, Connecticut. They had two children, Elizabeth and David.
51. His cemetery marker states that he died on September 7, 1783, at the age of twenty-six.
52. To add to the complexity, David Hale married his first cousin Laura Hale on January 18, 1815.
53. Holloway, *Nathan Hale*.
54. *Atlantic Monthly* 12 (December 1863): 665–79.
55. Robert Beverly Hale died as a young adult.
56. John Quincy Adams's son, Charles Francis, married a sister of Charlotte Brooks.

CHAPTER 5

57. Humphreys, *Life and Times*, vol. II, 424.

58. Ibid., vol. I, vi.

59. Ibid. The Constitution of 1818 removed the last vestige of the supremacy of the Congregational Churches.

60. Bushman, *From Puritan to Yankee*.

61. So eloquent that she was given the sobriquet of "Lady," which she enhanced to perfection.

62. Humphreys, *Life and Times*. Both the Humphrey and Humphreys surnames appear in family records. David opted for the latter spelling during and after the Revolution.

63. Joseph Moss White to Thomas Jefferson, January 1, 1801, National Archives. Humphrey's pamphlet was an enclosure.

64. Lawyer John (II) (1774–1826), Sally (1775–1812), Polly (1777–1848), Daniel (1779–1807), Anne (1781–1875), Susy (1783–1810), David (1786–1814) and Billy (1788–1877).

65. Orcutt, *History of the Old Town of Derby*.

66. Also known as the "Hartford Wits," this informal Yale literary group satirized their college curriculum, society and politics. Wordsmith Noah Webster has also been linked to the group.

67. Grizzard, *George!*, 154.

68. While accepting the presidency, Washington wanted to be certain to disavow any attempt at a political dynasty.

69. Humphreys, *Life and Times*, 358; Chernow, *Washington*, 474. Entitling his edits "Remarks," Washington carefully edited Humphreys's draft. Although he instructed his aide to burn or return the invaluable commentary, the eleven-page manuscript—documenting his experiences from late 1753 until 1758—was never destroyed.

70. Her father did business in Lisbon, Portugal.

71. Humphreys, *Life and Times*.

72. David Humphreys, *The Miscellaneous Works of David Humphreys* (1804).

CHAPTER 6

73. Elizabeth Backus is the daughter of Samuel Backus and Elizabeth Tracy and the granddaughter of Joseph Backus and Elizabeth Huntington.

74. Joshua and Zachariah were also officers during the war.

75. His wife's uncle Stephen Moore was the owner of West Point, New York, which, through the recommendation of General Huntington, was selected as the site of the U.S. military academy; Anne's father was a Loyalist.

76. McCrackan, *Huntington Letters*.

77. Ibid., 134.

78. A gravesite plaque lists the date of birth as 1738, while other sources state 1739.

79. The first portion is an unattributed quote, followed by the words of Benjamin Rush.

80. An office that then included the duties of chief judge of its Superior Court.

81. In 1660, his descendants were among members of a party that settled in Norwich, Connecticut; date of birth and spelling vary.

82. McCrackan, *Huntington Letters*, footnotes on 176–77.

83. Genealogists have determined that Franklin Delano Roosevelt was distantly related to a total of eleven U.S. presidents, five by blood and six by marriage: John Adams, John Quincy Adams, Ulysses Grant, William Henry Harrison, Benjamin Harrison, James Madison, Theodore Roosevelt, William Taft, Zachary Taylor, Martin Van Buren and George Washington. In Connecticut, however, we claim a total of twelve.

CHAPTER 7

84. William Beach's father, Isaac, married Hannah Birdseye in 1693 in Stratford, Connecticut.

85. The family of Samuel W. Johnson included Anna Francis, William Samuel, Sarah Elizabeth, Edward and Roland Charles.

86. The Verplancks of Fishkill, New York, were married on October 29, 1785. The couple had two children: Gulian Crommelin, who became a New York state assemblyman, and Ann, who died in infancy. Following Elizabeth's death, Verplanck remarried.

87. Robert C. Johnson had four children, some of whom were raised by the family of Samuel W. Johnson after 1806.
88. Johnson enjoyed close associations with the Anglican Church in England and with the scholarly community in Oxford, which awarded him an honorary degree in 1766.
89. Later, the Constitutional Convention would become Johnson's forum to alleviate all concern.

CHAPTER 8

90. Poet David Humphreys's description of Parsons in an epic poem.
91. Hall, *Life and Letters of Samuel Holden Parsons.*
92. Jonathan and Phebe Parsons had thirteen children, six of whom died in infancy.
93. The early history of Connecticut and the story of the Wolcott family are close to being the same thing.
94. Wolcott Jr. held the treasury role from 1795 until 1800. Hillhouse filled the vacancy caused by the resignation of Oliver Ellsworth. During the Sixth Congress, he was president pro tempore of the Senate.
95. Tactical acumen, which by all accounts was lacking, could not compensate for the overwhelming troop strength of the British, which was three times that of the Patriots. The response was unexpected: the Connecticut militia—already deserting in high numbers—were branded as cowards for running from the enemy.
96. Timothy Dwight IV, licensed to preach in 1777, was appointed chaplain in the Connecticut Continental Brigade of General Parsons. He inspired the troops with his sermons and the stirring war songs he composed, the most famous of which is "Columbia."
97. Hall, *Life and Letters.*
98. Ibid., 312–69.
99. Ibid.
100. In the appendix, he also includes letters from Charles J. McCurdy, Charles S. Hall and General William T. Sherman, who adds his veneration for the name Parsons.
101. Parsons had been fully vindicated in a paper read by Mr. J.G. Woodward before the Connecticut Historical Society in 1896.

CHAPTER 9

102. Trumbull, *True-Blue Laws of Connecticut and New Haven*, 31.

103. Peters, *Peters of New England*, 155. John was the founder of the Connecticut line and the only child of William and Margaret Russ. John and Mary were among the founding families of St. Peters Episcopal Church and strong supporters of the Crown.

104. Peters, *General History of Connecticut*, 262.

105. Trumbull, *Jonathan Trumbull*, 126.

106. Ibid.

107. Ibid. 128.

108. David Trumbull (1751–1822) was Jonathan and Faith Trumbull's third son. He served as commissary of the Colony of Connecticut. Reverend Benjamin Pomeroy, pastor of the Hebron Congregational Church, was a colonist sympathizer, and his intervention was later acknowledged.

109. Trumbull, *Jonathan Trumbull*, 131.

110. Peters lived briefly in Prairie du Chien, Wisconsin, before moving to New York City.

111. William and Polly "Patty" Marvin Jarvis, of Stamford, Connecticut, who were married on May 4, 1796, had nine children. Of the seven who survived infancy, Samuel Peters Jarvis became a prominent banker, developer, merchant and politician in New Orleans.

112. This was a well-publicized trial of traitors held in Ancaster, Ontario, from May until June 1814.

113. Bemslee Peters (1743–1798) was the twelfth child of John Peters and Mary Marks.

114. The Democrats and Whigs would dominate state politics for the next twenty years; those of note serving longer terms include Whig William W. Ellsworth (four years) and Democrat Thomas H. Seymour (three and a half years).

115. Peters, *Peters of New England*, 163.

116. A South Carolina landowner had sailed to Connecticut to claim the family.

117. The event would earn the town of Hebron a designation by the Amistad Committee in 2007 as part of the Connecticut Freedom Trail.

CHAPTER 10

118. White, *Bi-Centennial Celebration*, 60.
119. The Pierce family found their way to Litchfield through Farmington in the early 1750s. The Pierce ancestry traces back to John Pierce of England and that of the Pattersons to a prominent Scottish family from Dumfriesshire. James Patterson, born in Scotland, was one of the earliest settlers of Wethersfield and married Mary Talcot(t) on November 30, 1704. It is believed that his family was responsible for introducing tin to this country. Mary's father, Major John Paterson, was a distinguished colonial officer.
120. Vanderpoel, *Chronicles of a Pioneer School*, Appendix E
121. Ibid.
122. White, *Bi-Centennial Celebration*, 63. This source lists the name as Mary Goodman, per a recommendation by The Litchfield Historical Society, while others claim it was Mary Goodwin. Burial records were used to confirm dates.
123. Hollister's *History of Connecticut* quotes the lower figure and Mr. John P. Brace (1793–1872) the higher. While the academy was primarily for girls and young women, at least 125 boys are known to have attended.
124. White, *Bi-Centennial Celebration*, 65-66.
125. Miss Mary Pierce eventually purchased the academy property. It was then removed and used as a boys' school for a few years before being incorporated into a homestead. Mrs. Underwood, who purchased the property, tore down the Pierce residence in 1896.
126. Vanderpoel, *Chronicles of a Pioneer School*, 7.

CHAPTER 11

127. Pontiac's War (1763–66) was an American Indian struggle against British military occupation of the Great Lakes region.
128. Legend has included him not changing clothes, mounting a horse in a nearby stable and riding to consult with other militia officers, committee members and even Governor Trumbull.
129. Putnam was with the force commanded by Colonel William Prescott and that, on the night of June 16, fortified Breed's Hill. Following the Battle of Bunker Hill, Putnam occupied the strategic Prospect Hill.

130. Hill, *Life of Israel Putnam*, 265. Joachim Murat (1767–1815) earned a reputation as a gifted and daring cavalry leader.
131. Thomas Putnam, half brother to Joseph, was a significant accuser during the trials and even levied assertions against members of the Porter family.
132. Her father, William Hawthorne III, came to this country in 1630; Nathaniel Hawthorne was a lineal descendant.
133. The Putnam family also had servants.
134. Sources vary; headstone at South Cemetery in Brooklyn, Connecticut.
135. Ibid.
136. Ibid.
137. Ibid.
138. Ibid.
139. A plaque marks the former location of "The General Wolfe."
140. Sources vary on date of birth.
141. In 1849, author Richard Frothingham claimed William Prescott was in charge at the time of the battle.
142. Historians from that era, including William Gordon, David Humphreys, John Marshall and Mercy Otis Warren, do not mention it.
143. This caused the eventual removal of the mutilated stone for safekeeping at the Connecticut State Capitol in Hartford. Israel Putnam's remains were removed from the cemetery in 1888 and placed in a sarcophagus built into the foundation of a monument erected on a plot of ground near the Brooklyn town green. On top of this stirring monument stands an equestrian statue of one of the state's greatest heroes.

CHAPTER 12

144. In 1933, a publication by the Connecticut Tercentenary Commission dated the period as being from 1776 to 1833. William and Mary believes it holds the honor of being the first law school in America; "the first not associated with a college or university" was the 1960s claim by the U.S. Department of the Interior.
145. Aaron Burr lived with his brother-in-law.
146. James Gould, a former student, joined Reeve in 1798. Over one thousand law students graduated before the school closed in 1833.
147. Gould took over the school at this point, as Reeve's voice was failing.

148. Reeve's *Law of Baron and Femme*, first published in 1816, was the preeminent American treatise on family law for much of the nineteenth century.
149. Beecher, *Autobiography of Lyman Beecher*, 233, 373.
150. Burr was cared for briefly by his grandparents.
151. Todd, *General History of the Burr Family*, 120.
152. Ibid., 93.
153. Ibid., 124. Later, Burr's fidelity would be questioned.
154. Burr tried every means possible to obtain information, but nothing was heard of the vessel.
155. Charles Burr Todd noted, "His object was, as he said, to make himself master of Mexico, and place himself at the head of it, and if they had let him alone he would have done it." Todd, *General History of the Burr Family*, 122–23.
156. Ibid., 127.
157. As one might surmise, it certainly doesn't hurt to have had John Marshall, Thomas Jefferson or James Monroe as students.

CHAPTER 13

158. Under the pseudonym "A Countryman," he wrote a series of newspaper letters to the people of Connecticut supporting the Constitution.
159. Sherman's family had moved to Stoughton, Massachusetts, in 1723; Roger's father was a farmer.
160. His Harvard-trained parish minister was Reverend Samuel Danbar.
161. Sherman became an attorney and was admitted to the bar in 1754.
162. Roger Sherman moved to New Haven, Connecticut, on June 30, 1761. Instead of practicing law, he engaged in mercantile pursuits.
163. The three eldest sons served as officers during the Revolution.
164. Sources have varied regarding this date.
165. Sherman, *Sherman Genealogy*, 206.
166. Root, *Chapter Sketches*, 39.
167. Reference made by Katharine Prescott Bennett in the *Journal of American History*.
168. Root, *Chapter Sketches*, 39.
169. Additional noteworthy descendants include editor Maxwell "Max" Perkins and Watergate prosecutor Archibald Cox Jr., among others.

170. His son, Simeon Eben Baldwin (1840–1927), was also governor of Connecticut (1911–15).
171. Adams, *Correspondence*, 1809.
172. His compromise on representation in Congress broke the "deadlock" between large and small states.
173. Boutell, *Life of Roger Sherman*, 291.
174. ALS to Sanderson's Biographies, November 19, 1822; Boutell, *Life of Roger Sherman*, 291.

CHAPTER 14

175. Tallmadge, *Memoir*, 43.
176. Heitman, *Historical Register of Officers*. Samuel did not attend college. Though it is unclear, John might also have served.
177. Benjamin was a very good friend of Connecticut Patriot Nathan Hale.
178. A position offered by Captain John Chester of Wethersfield.
179. Tallmadge, *Memoir*, 11.
180. Ibid., 22. Congress had resolved to raise eighty-eight battalions of infantry through state quotas.
181. Ibid., 49 "Having constant and repeated intelligence from New York, and all parts of Long Island, I began to entertain the plan of breaking up the whole [British] system."
182. Benjamin Tallmadge to Reverend Manasseh Cutler, January 11, 1800.
183. Mary Floyd, Cornelia, Benjamin, Montgomery and Henry. Laura Tallmadge (1814–1816) died young.
184. Sources vary; Cushman had attended the Litchfield Law School in 1808.
185. Harriet, Tallmadge, Clarence and Mary.
186. Tallmadge, *Memoir*, 145.

Chapter 15

187. Believed to be on January 31, 1705 or 1706.
188. Reverend Robinson bought his new son-in-law, Jonathan Trumbull, two tracts of land in Goshen Parish. Jonathan Trumbull's home, now a National Historic Landmark, was built by his father and originally located near the intersection of Route 207 and West Town Street.
189. Joseph Trumbull died insolvent and without children on July 23, 1778.
190. On January 5, 1785, his widow married Colonel Hezekiah Wyllys.
191. American National Biography; *Dictionary of American Biography*; Ifkovic, *Connecticut's Nationalist Revolutionary*.
192. Trumbull, *Jonathan Trumbull*, 30.
193. Ibid., 174.
194. Jedidiah Huntington returned to Norwich following the war and distinguished himself in a variety of civic and religious roles. His second wife was Anne Moore, daughter of a New York businessman.
195. Colonel Williams willed funds for a college that would later become Williams College in Williamstown, Massachusetts.
196. Governor Trumbull was elected to that honor on March 17, 1784. General Washington was the first president-general of the society.
197. Governor Trumbull's farewell address has often been compared to Washington's address to the governors of the thirteen states.
198. Ibid.
199. Trumbull, *Jonathan Trumbull*, 334–35.
200. Ibid; George Washington to Jonathan Trumbull Jr., October 1, 1785.

Chapter 16

201. *American Dictionary of the English Language* (1828).
202. Noah Jr. was the great-great-grandson of John Webster, one of Hartford's original settlers, and the great-great-great-grandson of Governor William Bradford.
203. According to Yale University.
204. Scudder, *Noah Webster*, 7. In the autumn of 1777, Noah enlisted as a private in his father's unit, which was on its way to resist General Burgoyne.

205. Webster's Yale class of 1778 was considered the most distinguished up until the Civil War.
206. Some sources note that Webster failed to be admitted to the bar in Litchfield.
207. Scudder, *Noah Webster*, 10.
208. Webster received his MA from Yale in September 1781.
209. Scudder, *Noah Webster*, 33.
210. She died twenty-three days after giving birth.
211. Louisa was referred to as a spinster in Ford, *Notes on the Life of Noah Webster*.
212. Ford, *Notes on the Life of Noah Webster*, 507.
213. *A Collection of Essays and Fugitive Writings*, "Woman's Education in the Last Century" by Noah Webster, 1790.
214. Later, George and Charles Merriam purchased the rights to this dictionary from Webster's estate.
215. Noah Webster to George Washington, 1785, Noah Webster Manuscript, New York Public Library.
216. Warfel, *Schoolmaster to America*.

Chapter 17

217. There is a discrepancy in a number of accounts of Oliver Wolcott's life as to his date of birth. Some sources list his birth date as November 20, while others state December 1, 1726. This discrepancy is caused by the change from the Julian to Gregorian calendar, the latter of which was adopted in the American colonies in 1752.
218. The Treaty of Aix-la-Chapelle formally ended the war, but the outstanding territorial issues still existed.
219. Gibbs, *Memoirs of the Administrations*, 9. Gibbs was the son-in-law of Oliver Wolcott Jr.
220. The *National Encyclopedia of American Biography* termed her "thrifty" and "energetic."
221. William Wolcott Ellsworth, the twin brother of Henry Leavitt, married another of Noah Webster's daughters. After Webster's death, Chauncey Allen Goodrich edited his famous dictionary.
222. Henry Wolcott was born in 1578 in Tolland, Somerset, England.
223. Two daughters, Anna and Mary, were left behind with their brother. They would join their parents in Windsor around 1640.

224. This was in response to a general call by Massachusetts governor William Shirley to the New England colonies; Wolcott was under the leadership of Sir William Pepperrell.

225. General Wolcott would later take the bullets to Saratoga, where he and his militia helped defeat the British army under General Burgoyne.

CHAPTER 18

226. Deming, *An Oration*.

227. Ibid.

228. Ibid.

229. In 1739.

230. A congressional delegation led by Benjamin Franklin was unable to garner Canadian support of the rebellion against Great Britain. This led to a controversial "legal" plunder from area merchants and numerous accusations.

231. After the war, Thomas Wooster went with his family to New Orleans. Returning from a New Haven business trip, his ship was lost at sea.

232. Ogden was bitter that the Wooster family did not retain the Connecticut collector's office post and blamed it on the Trumbull and Wolcott families.

233. A February 7, 1799 letter from Ogden to Thomas Jefferson states a few of the opinions he held later in life. It can be found in the National Archives.

234. The brothers, Henry and David, each had a son named after them. It was these two sons, or Wooster cousins, who were among the band that took part in the notorious local kidnapping case of Chauncey Judd on March 15, 1780.

235. The Wooster insolvency was partially a result of paying his troops from his personal funds.

236. Orcutt, *History of the Old Town of Derby*, 671.

237. Deming, *An Oration*, 59.

BIBLIOGRAPHY

Please note: Records, including those of birth, marriage and death, can vary significantly from source to source. Also, the British Empire (including the eastern part of what is now the United States) adopted the Gregorian calendar in 1752, by which time it was necessary to correct by eleven days.

ARTICLES

Baker, Edward. "Benedict Arnold Turns and Burns New London." http:// norwichhistoricalsociety.org/news/documents/NHSNewsletterFall2013.pdf.

Bissell, F.C. "The Reverend Samuel Peters, L.L.D., of Hebron, Connecticut, Loyalist, His Slaves and Their Near Abduction." 1787. http://www. hebronhistoricalsociety.org/images/slavery/Abduction_of_Peters_ Slaves__by_F_C_Bissell18991.pdf.

McCall, Donna J. "The Abduction, Rescue, and Emancipation of Cesar and Lowis Peters." http://www.hebronhistoricalsociety.org/images/ slavery/Abduction_Rescue__Emancipation_of_Cesar__Lowis__vl2.pdf.

Peter, Courtney. "The Oliver Ellsworth Homestead: The Pleasantest Place in Windsor." http://www.ctdar.org/forms/EllsworthHome.pdf

Swindler, William F. "America's First Law Schools: Significance or Chauvinism?" *Connecticut Bar Journal* 2, no. 4 (1967).

WEBSITES

Ancestry.com. http://www.ancestry.com.

The Connecticut Society of the Daughters of the American Revolution. http://www.dar.org.

The Connecticut Society of the Sons of the American Revolution. http://. www.sar.org.

The Courant/Connecticut Courant. http://www.courant.com.

Dictionary of Canadian Biography. http://www.biographi.ca.

Hale Collection of Connecticut Cemetery Records. http://www.hale-collection.com.

The History of the Old Town of Derby, Connecticut, 1641–1880. http:// dunhamwilcox.net/ct/derby_ct1.htm.

Hog River Journal. http://www.hogriver.org.

Library of Congress. http://www.loc.gov.

New England Historic Genealogical Society. http://www.americanancestros.org.

Oliver Ellsworth Homestead. http://www.ellsworthhomesteaddar.org.

The Society of Cincinnati. http://www.societyofthecincinnati.org.

Wikipedia. http://www.wikipedia.org.

William C. Clements Library, Manuscript Division, University of Michigan. http://quod.ib.umich.edu.

Books

Adams, John. *Correspondence of the Late President Adams, Originally Published in the Boston Patriot in a Series of Letters.* Boston: Everett & Munroe, 1809.

Beecher, Charles, editor. *Autobiography, Correspondence, etc., of Lyman Beecher, D.D. Vol. I.* New York: Harper & Brothers, Publishers, 1865.

Boutell, Lewis Henry. *The Life of Roger Sherman.* Chicago: A.C. McClurg and Company, 1896.

Brown, Kathleen M. *Good Wives, Nasty Wenches and Anxious Patriarchs: Gender, Race and Power in Colonial Virginia.* Chapel Hill: University of North Carolina Press, 1996.

Bushman, Richard L. *From Puritan to Yankee: Character and the Social Order in Connecticut, 1690–1765.* Cambridge, MA: Harvard University Press, 1967.

Chernow, Ron. *Washington: A Life.* New York: Penguin Press, 2010.

Child, Franks S. *An Historic Mansion, Being an Account of the Thaddeus Burr Homestead.* Fairfield, CT: privately published, 1915.

Cutter, William Richard. *Genealogical and Family History of the State of Connecticut: A Record of the Achievements of Her People in the Making of a Commonwealth and the Founding of a Nation.* New York: Lewis Publishing Company, 1911.

Deetz, James, and Patricia Scott Deetz. *The Times of Their Lives: Life, Love, and Death in Plymouth Colony.* New York: W.H. Freeman and Co., 2000.

Deming, Henry Champion. *An Oration Upon the Life and Services of Gen. David Wooster, Delivered at Danbury, April 27*[th], *1854, When a Monument was Erected to His Memory*. Hartford, CT: Press of Case, Tiffany and Company, 1854.

Elkins, Stanle, and Eric McKitrick. *The Age of Federalism*. New York: Oxford University Press, 1993.

Ford, Emily Ellsworth Fowler. *Notes on the Life of Noah Webster*. Edited by Emily Ellsworth Ford Skeel. New York: privately printed, 1912.

Fox-Genovese, Elizabeth. *Within the Plantation Household: Black and White Women of the Old South*. Chapel Hill: University of North Carolina Press, 1988.

Friedman, Lawrence M. *A History of American Law*. New York: Simon & Schuster, 1985.

Gibbs, George. *Memoirs of the Administrations of Washington and John Adams: Edited from the Papers of Oliver Wolcott, Secretary of the Treasury*. 2 vols. New York: Printed for the Subscribers, 1846.

Greven, Philip. *The Protestant Temperament: Patterns of Child-Rearing, Religious Experience, and the Self in Early America*. Chicago: University of Chicago Press, 1988.

Grizzard, Frank E., Jr. *George! A Guide to All Things Washington*. Charlottesville, VA: Mariner, 2005.

Hall, Charles S. *Life and Letters of Samuel Holden Parsons*. Binghamton, NY: Otseningo Publishing Co., 1905.

Heitman, F.B. *Historical Register of Officers of the Continental Army during the War of the Revolution, April, 1775, to December, 1783*. Washington, D.C.: 1892.

Hill, George Canning. *The Life of Israel Putnam*. Edited with notes by Henry Ketcham. New York: A.L. Burt, 1903.

Holloway, Charlotte Molyneux. *Nathan Hale: The Martyr-Hero of the Revolution, with a Hale Genealogy and Hale's Diary*. New York: A.L. Burt, 1899.

Humphreys, Colonel David. *The Life and Heroic Exploits of Israel Putnam, Major-General in the Revolutionary War*. Hartford, CT: Silas Andrus and Son, 1847.

Humphreys, Frank Landon. *Life and Times of David Humphreys: Soldier—Statesman—Poet*. 2 vols. New York: G.P. Putnam's Sons, 1917.

Ifkovic, John. *Connecticut's Nationalist Revolutionary: Jonathan Trumbull, Jr.* Hartford: American Revolution Bicentennial Commission of Connecticut, 1977.

Johnston, Henry Phelps. *Nathan Hale 1776: Biography and Memorials*. New Haven, CT: Yale University Press, 1914.

Kilbourn, Dwight C. *The Bench and Bar of Litchfield County, Connecticut, 1709–1909*. Litchfield, CT: self-published, 1909.

Loring, George B. *A Vindication of General Samuel Holden Parsons, Against the Charge of Treasonable Correspondence During the Revolutionary War*. Salem, MA: Salem Press, 1888.

McCrackan, W.D., ed. *The Huntington Letters: In the Possession of Julie Chester Wells*. New York: Appleton Press, 1897.

McCullough, David. *John Adams*. New York: Simon & Schuster, 2001.

———. *1776*. New York: Simon & Schuster, 2005.

Mintz, Steven, and Susan Kellogg. *Domestic Revolutions: A Social History of American Family Life*. New York: Free Press, 1988.

Morgan, Edmund S. *The Puritan Family: Religion and Domestic Relations in Seventeenth-Century New England*. New York: Harper & Row, 1966.

Orcutt, Samuel. *The History of the Old Town of Derby, Connecticut, 1642–1880*. Springfield, MA: Press of Springfield Printing Company, 1880.

Peters, Edmund Frank. *Peters of New England: A Genealogy and Family History*. New York: Knickerbocker Press, 1903.

Raphael, Ray. *Founding Myths: Stories That Hide Our Patriotic Past.* New York: MJF Books, 2004.

Root, Mary Philotheta, ed. *Chapter Sketches, Connecticut Daughters of the American Revolution.* New Haven: Connecticut Daughters of the American Revolution, 1901.

Scudder, Horace E. *American Men of Letters: Noah Webster.* Boston: Houghton, Mifflin and Co., 1886.

Sherman, Thomas Townsend. *Sherman Genealogy.* New York: Tobias A. Wright, 1920.

Tallmadge, Benjamin. *Memoir of Col. Benjamin Tallmadge, Prepared by Himself, at the Request of His Children.* New York: Thomas Holman Book and Job Printer, 1858.

Talmadge, Arthur White. *The Talmadge, Tallmadge and Talmage Genealogy, Being the Descendants of Thomas Talmadge of Lynn, Massachusetts.* New York: Grafton Press, 1909.

Tarbox, Increase N. *Life of Israel Putnam.* Boston: Lockwood, Brooks and Company, 1876.

Todd, Charles Burr. *A General History of the Burr Family in America.* New York: E. Wells Sackett & Bro., 1878.

Trumbull, J. Hammond, ed. *The True-Blue Laws of Connecticut and New Haven and the False Blue-Laws Invented by Rev. Samuel Peters, to Which Were Added Specimens of the Law and Judicial Proceedings of Other Colonies and Some Blue-Laws of England in the Reign of James I.* Hartford, CT: American Publishing Company, 1876.

Trumbull, John. *Autobiography, Reminiscences and Letters of John Trumbull, from 1756 to 1841.* New York: Wiley and Putnam, 1841.

Trumbull, Jonathan. *Jonathan Trumbull, Governor of Connecticut, 1769–1784.* Boston: Little, Brown and Co., 1919.

Ulrich, Laurel Thatcher. *Good Wives: Image and Reality in the Lives of Women in Northern New England, 1650–1750.* New York: Vintage, 1991.

Vanderpoel, Emily Noyes, comp. *Chronicles of a Pioneer School, from 1792 to 1833: Being the History of Miss Sarah Pierce and Her Litchfield School.* Cambridge, UK: Cambridge University Press, 1903.

Warfel, Harry R. *Noah Webster: Schoolmaster to America.* New York: MacMillan Company, 1936.

White, Alain C. *The Bi-Centennial Celebration of the Settlement of Litchfield, Connecticut, August 1–4, 1920.* Compiled by the Litchfield Historical Society. Litchfield, CT: Enquirer Print, 1920.

Whittemore, Henry. *Our New England Ancestors and Their Descendants, 1620–1900: Historical, Genealogical, Biographical.* New York: New England Ancestral Publishing Company, 1900.

Wooster, David. *Genealogy of the Woosters in America: Descended from Edward Wooster of Connecticut.* San Francisco, CA: M. Weiss, 1885.

INDEX

ABOUT THE AUTHOR

Mark Allen Baker is a former business executive (assistant to the president and CEO at General Electric/Genigraphics Corporation, now Microsoft PowerPoint) and entrepreneur. As the author of eighteen books—including the award-nominated *Title Town USA: Boxing in Upstate New York*, *Basketball*  *History in Syracuse: Hoops Roots* and *Spies of Revolutionary Connecticut: From Benedict Arnold to Nathan Hale*—and a historian, his expertise has been referenced in numerous periodicals, including *USA TODAY*, *Sports Illustrated* and *Money*. Baker has appeared on numerous radio and television shows, including serving as a co-host on *Rock Collectors*, a VH1 television series.

The author can be contacted at: P.O. Box 782, Hebron, CT, 06248.